Clinical Lectures
on Klein and Bion

The New Library of Psychoanalysis was launched in 1987 in association with the Institute of Psycho-Analysis, London. Its purpose is to facilitate a greater and more widespread appreciation of what psychoanalysis is really about and to provide a forum for increasing mutual understanding between psychoanalysts and those working in other disciplines such as history, linguistics, literature, medicine, philosophy, psychology, and the social sciences. It is intended that the titles selected for publication in the series should deepen and develop psychoanalytic thinking and technique, contribute to psychoanalysis from outside, or contribute to other disciplines from a psychoanalytical perspective.

The Institute, together with the British Psycho-Analytical Society, runs a low-fee psychoanalytic clinic, organizes lectures and scientific events concerned with psychoanalysis, publishes the *International Journal of Psycho-Analysis* and the *International Review of Psycho-Analysis*, and runs the only training course in the UK in psychoanalysis leading to membership of the International Psychoanalytical Association – the body which preserves internationally agreed standards of training, of professional entry, and of professional ethics and practice for psychoanalysis as initiated and developed by Sigmund Freud. Distinguished members of the Institute have included Michael Balint, Wilfred Bion, Ronald Fairbairn, Anna Freud, Ernest Jones, Melanie Klein, John Rickman, and Donald Winnicott.

Volumes 1–11 in the series have been prepared under the general editorship of David Tuckett, with Ronald Britton and Eglé Laufer as associate editors. Subsequent volumes are under the general editorship of Elizabeth Bott Spillius, with Christopher Bollas, David Taylor, and Rosine Jozef Perelberg as associate editors.

IN THE SAME SERIES

1 *Impasse and Interpretation* Herbert Rosenfeld

2 *Psychoanalysis and Discourse* Patrick Mahony

3 *The Suppressed Madness of Sane Men* Marion Milner

4 *The Riddle of Freud* Estelle Roith

5 *Thinking, Feeling, and Being* Ignacio Matte-Blanco

6 *The Theatre of the Dream* Salomon Resnik

7 *Melanie Klein Today: Volume 1, Mainly Theory*
Edited by Elizabeth Bott Spillius

8 *Melanie Klein Today: Volume 2, Mainly Practice*
Edited by Elizabeth Bott Spillius

9 *Psychic Equilibrium and Psychic Change: Selected Papers of Betty Joseph*
Edited by Michael Feldman and Elizabeth Bott Spillius

10 *About Children and Children-No-Longer: Collected Papers 1942–80*
Paula Heimann. Edited by Margret Tonnesmann

11 *The Freud–Klein Controversies 1941–45*
Edited by Pearl King and Riccardo Steiner

12 *Dream, Phantasy and Art* Hanna Segal

13 *Psychic Experience and Problems of Technique* Harold Stewart

NEW LIBRARY OF PSYCHOANALYSIS
14

General editor: Elizabeth Bott Spillius

Clinical Lectures on Klein and Bion

Edited by
ROBIN ANDERSON

Foreword by Hanna Segal

TAVISTOCK/ROUTLEDGE
LONDON AND NEW YORK

First published in 1992
by Routledge
11 New Fetter Lane, London EC4P 4EE

Simultaneously published in the USA and Canada
by Routledge
a division of Routledge, Chapman and Hall Inc.
29 West 35th Street, New York, NY 10001

Typeset by LaserScript, Mitcham, Surrey.
Printed and bound in Great Britain by
Mackays of Chatham PLC, Chatham, Kent

British Library Cataloguing in Publication Data
Clinical lectures on Klein and Bion. – (The New Library of
psychoanalysis, v. 14).
1. Psychoanalysis. Klein, Melanie 1882–1960. Bion, Wilfred R.
(Wilfred Ruprecht) 1897–1979
I. Anderson, Robin II. Series
150.195

Library of Congress Cataloging in Publication Data
Clinical lectures on Klein and Bion/edited by Robin Anderson:
foreword by Hanna Segal.
p. cm. – (New library of psychoanalysis: 14)
Includes bibliographical references.
Includes index.
1. Psychoanalysis. 2. Klein, Melanie. 3. Bion, Wilfred R.
(Wilfred Ruprecht), 1897–1979. I. Anderson, Robin, 1941–   .
II. Series
[DNLM: 1. Klein, Melanie. 2. Bion, Wilfred R. (Wilfred Ruprecht),
1897–1979. 3. Psychoanalysis. W1 NE455G v. 14/WM 460 C6405]
RC480.5C554 1992
616.89′17 – dc20
DLC
for Library of Congress   91-532
CIP

ISBN 0–415–06992–0
0–415–06993–9 (pbk)

Contents

List of contributors   vii

Foreword by Hanna Segal   ix

Acknowledgement   xi

Introduction *Robin Anderson*   1

1   Child analysis and the concept of unconscious phantasy *Patricia Daniel*   14

2   The emergence of early object relations in the psychoanalytic setting *Irma Brenman Pick*   24

3   The Oedipus situation and the depressive position *Ronald Britton*   34

4   The equilibrium between the paranoid-schizoid and the depressive positions *John Steiner*   46

5   Clinical experiences of projective identification *Elizabeth Bott Spillius*   59

6   Splitting and projective identification *Michael Feldman*   74

7   Psychosis: not thinking in a bizarre world *Edna O'Shaughnessy*   89

8   Keeping things in mind *Ronald Britton*   102

9   As if: the phenomenon of not learning *Ruth Riesenberg Malcolm*   114

References   126

Name index   134

Subject index   136

Contributors

All the contributors are training analysts of the British Psycho-Analytical Society and are or have been actively involved in teaching and the organization of training as well as in the analysis and supervision of candidates.

Dr Robin Anderson, (M.B., B.S., M.R.C.P., M.R.C. Psych.) is a child and adult psychoanalyst in part-time private psychoanalytic practice and is Chairman of the Adolescent Department of the Tavistock Clinic, London.

Dr Ronald Britton (M.B., B.S., F.R.C. Psych., D.P.M.&H., D.P.M.) is in full-time private psychoanalytic practice. He was formerly the Chairman of the Department for Children and Parents at the Tavistock Clinic, London.

Miss Patricia Daniel (Soc. Sci. Dip.) is now in full-time private psychoanalytic practice. She was formerly Deputy Director of Social Services in an Inner London Borough and subsequently part-time Principal in Social Work, Adult Department, Tavistock Clinic.

Dr Michael Feldman (B.A., M.B., B.S., M.R.C.P., M.Phil., F.R.C. Psych.) is in part-time private psychoanalytic practice and is also Consultant Psychotherapist at the Maudsley Hospital, London.

Mrs Ruth Riesenberg Malcolm (B.A.) is in full-time private psychoanalytic practice. She formerly created and organized the Department of Social Work in the University of Chile Medical School Psychiatric Clinic. Later at the same clinic she developed the child psychology and child analysis service.

Mrs Edna O'Shaughnessy (B.A., B.Phil.) is a child and adult psychoanalyst and is in full-time private psychoanalytic practice. Formerly she was also Lecturer in the Department of Child Development, Institute of Education, London.

Mrs Irma Brenman Pick (B.A.) is a child and adult psychoanalyst and is in full-time private practice.

Mrs Elizabeth Bott Spillius (Ph.D.) is now in full-time private psychoanalytic practice. Formerly she was a social anthropologist (*Family and Social Network: Tongan Society at the Time of Captain Cook's Visits*). She edited volumes 7 and 8 of the present series and is now General Editor of the series.

Dr John Steiner (M.B., Ch.B., Ph.D., F.R.C.Psych., D.P.M.) is in part-time private psychoanalytic practice and is also Consultant Psychotherapist, Adult Department, Tavistock Clinic. He has a special interest in borderline patients. Formerly he was Chairman of the Association for Psychoanalytic Psychotherapy in the National Health Service.

Foreword

HANNA SEGAL

This book is based on nine papers originally given in a series of public lectures intended to acquaint a large, mixed audience with some developments in psychoanalytic thinking and practice. One could say that they were meant to 'popularize' psychoanalysis.

Popularization can be only too easy. One can present 'Klein and Bion without tears in eight easy lessons'. It can be done by making disturbing discoveries seem anodyne, deep and complex thought appear easily understandable and acceptable when sufficiently watered down.

The editor and authors of the chapters in this collection set themselves a far more daunting task, that of making ideas understandable without denuding them of any of their meaning. They do not talk down to their audiences; they try to make them participate in some of their experience. And they treat the work of Klein and Bion with respect and integrity: not avoiding what is disturbing and not making superficial or easy what is deep and complex.

In each of the chapters the authors give briefly a theoretical formulation of the concepts they wish to present, and then at much greater length they show in depth and detail how they use them in their work. Any conviction that the audience may derive about the validity of these concepts will not be based on arguments, but on the impact of the actual work presented by the psychoanalyst. Conclusions are left to the listener's or reader's own imagination.

After a comprehensive general introduction, the first chapter introduces the reader to Klein's usage of the concept of unconscious phantasy, central to all her work. The remaining authors then illustrate several of Klein's other central ideas. Cumulatively the six chapters on Klein not only give a vivid picture of the meaning and import of these concepts, but also of the extent to which they have been enriched and developed since Klein first formulated them. For instance, nearly all the chapters tackle some aspects of projective identification – a mechanism Klein describes in only a few lines in her paper 'Notes on some schizoid mechanisms'.

The three chapters on Bion show the development of Klein's ideas on projective identification into his theory of the interaction between the container and the contained, and his exploration of the whole area of the human capacity to think, together with the differentiation between psychotic and non-psychotic functioning which is largely dependent on this interaction. Each of these chapters shows a different aspect of what it is like to live in a mad world. As in the case of the chapters on Klein they make no attempt to present in a simplified form the whole of Bion's work; the authors take us in to their consulting rooms and give us a glimpse of the patient's world and their own understanding of it, helped by Bion's insights. And each author has his or her individual approach and extends Klein's and Bion's work further.

Because of this approach, even though the chapters were first given as public lectures the book can be seen as a sequel of *Melanie Klein Today*, numbers 7 and 8 of the New Library of Psychoanalysis. They show a further development of work based on Klein and, though some of the authors contributed also to *Melanie Klein Today*, some are new (Anderson, Britton, Daniel, Feldman). These chapters bear witness to the continued vitality and growth of Klein's ideas.

Acknowledgement

I am grateful to Elizabeth Bott Spillius for all her help and guidance in the preparation of this book.

Introduction

ROBIN ANDERSON

The first six chapters of this book are devoted to the work of Melanie Klein. They, like the three chapters on the work of Wilfred Bion, are based on a series of 'Public Lecture Days' or conferences held at the Institute of Psycho-Analysis in London. The first 'Klein Day' consisted of lectures by Patricia Daniel, Ronald Britton, and Michael Feldman, the second of lectures by Irma Brenman Pick, John Steiner, and Elizabeth Bott Spillius. The 'Bion Day' included lectures by Edna O'Shaughnessy, Ruth Riesenberg Malcolm, and Ronald Britton. These open lectures are intended to bring psychoanalysis to the attention of a wider public. The particular lectures published here were not meant to give a comprehensive view of Klein's or Bion's works, but instead were intended to present some of their more interesting and important ideas in a clinically alive way to those relatively unfamiliar with them. The emphasis therefore has been to show how the ideas and theories are used in practice by analysts working now. The lectures show how some of Klein's original ideas are used today in much the same way as she used them, while others have been developed and modified – evidence that psychoanalysis is, as it should be, a living science and method of treatment. Because the lectures were intended to concern specifically the ideas of Klein and Bion, most of the authors make little attempt to discuss the ideas of other current psychoanalysts on the topics addressed.

Accounts of Melanie Klein's life may be found in Segal (1979) and Grosskurth (1986). A general introduction to her ideas will be found in Segal (1973). Hinshelwood (1989) presents a comprehensive dictionary of Kleinian concepts which is especially helpful on Klein's early ideas. Spillius (1988) has collected and commented on a series of papers written between 1950 and 1988 by British followers of Klein, showing some of the changes and continuities in their usage of her

1

ideas. There have been many critiques of Klein's work by both British analysts and American ego psychologists; these are well summarized by Kernberg (1969), and Yorke (1971) and Greenson (1974) have subsequently added their own critiques. Klein's work is gradually becoming better known and has been summarized and commented on by several authors, for example Greenberg and Mitchell (1983), Frosh (1987), Hughes (1989).

Melanie Klein (née Reizes) was born in Vienna in 1882, the daughter of a struggling doctor. Most of her childhood was spent in Vienna where, interestingly, despite her cultural interests she never came across Freud, reflecting perhaps the very small psychoanalytic community in the early years of this century. She was in her thirties before she discovered psychoanalysis. She married young and seems to have sacrificed the possibility of university for the sake of her marriage. The marriage was not a happy one and did not fulfil her, and moreover on account of her husband's work she was forced to live in very small provincial towns with little cultural stimulation so that she felt isolated and deprived of the intellectual life she had had in Vienna. In 1910 she moved to Budapest, then a thriving and important city at the heart of the Austro-Hungarian empire, where there was an important psycho-analytic group. Here she discovered Freud – she read his paper 'On dreams' and was captivated. She wrote of that time, 'that was what I was aiming at, at least during those years when I was so very keen to find what would satisfy me intellectually and emotionally' (Grosskurth 1986: 69). She went into analysis with Ferenczi, partly because of her interest, but also because she felt the need for help. Ferenczi was impressed with her and encouraged her especially in her work with children which was quite new at that time. She moved to Berlin in 1921 and Abraham, her teacher and later her analyst, encouraged and supported her. His own interests were very much concerned with the early infantile processes that he had detected in his patients. Klein's work with young children supported and added to his ideas. She very much needed his protection as her ideas were already causing much controversy in Berlin. When he died in 1925 her position there became much more difficult. Part of the problem was that the Berlin Society looked to Vienna very much as the fountain-head of psycho-analysis, where of course Anna Freud was also working with children on a very different basis. So Klein found herself more and more isolated in Berlin. In England on the other hand there was more independence from Vienna and there had in any case already been interest in her work. Jones and others were studying early infantile development and primitive mental life, and Alix Strachey, who had encountered Klein

2

in Berlin (Meisel and Kendrick 1986), was instrumental in encouraging her to give lectures in London in 1925, which proved to be very popular and led to her decision to settle in London.

Klein wrote of that time:

> In 1925 I had the wonderful experience of speaking to an interested and appreciative audience in London. All members were present at Dr Stephens' house. ... The three weeks I spent in London were one of the happiest times of my life. I found such friendliness, hospitality and interest and I developed a great liking for the English. It is true that later on things did not always go so easily but those three weeks were very important in my decision to live in England.
>
> (Grosskurth 1986: 157)

She quickly established herself in the British Society and continued to develop her ideas of early mental life, drawing especially on her work with children. At first these ideas very much followed Freud and Abraham (see Chapter 1) but by the mid-1930s she had begun to develop ideas that were more uniquely her own. They were quite radical and challenging and inevitably led to disagreements within the British Society and this escalated after the arrival of the Viennese analysts, especially Anna Freud with her father, all fleeing Nazi persecution. (An account of the Freud–Klein controversies, 1941–45, will be found in King and Steiner 1990.)

Despite these differences the British Society held together and Klein continued to develop her ideas and extend her theories right until the end of her life. Her work on envy was published when she was in her mid-seventies. She died in 1960 within days of reading the final proofs of her last work, fittingly on the analysis of a child, 'Richard', called *The Narrative of a Child Analysis* (1960).

A central feature of Klein's contribution to psychoanalysis is that it began in the study and treatment of children. She developed the play technique (Klein 1955), which opened up a whole new world of empathic understanding of small children's feelings and phantasies. Klein was at first distressed by the very aggressive and violent nature of some of the phantasies of these small children, just as an earlier generation had been shocked by Freud's understanding of infantile sexuality. Encouraged by Abraham and stimulated by Freud's discoveries and conceptualizations, perhaps especially *The Ego and the Id* (Freud 1923a), she was soon confidently discovering that even very small children had a very early and severe superego which she explained as the result of the projection of their own violent impulses into the mother and father, the 'primary objects' (Klein 1927; 1928).

She placed increasing emphasis on introjection and projection in psychic development, and developed new views on symbol formation and how it could become inhibited by anxiety (Klein 1930).

The first chapter of the present book, 'Child analysis and the concept of unconscious phantasy' by Patricia Daniel, begins with a brief account of Klein's technique of child analysis and the way in which this new method allowed her to build on the work of Freud and others, especially Abraham. It focuses especially on her ideas on introjection and the development of the concept of an internal world derived from processes of projection and introjection. Daniel describes the way Klein links this with primitive oral and anal phantasies of the mother's body and its contents, leading to a detailed discussion of unconscious phantasy and symbolism, on which all later developmental processes, such as the Oedipus complex (see Chapter 3), are based. Daniel illustrates these ideas with clinical examples from both Klein's writings and her own work, using mainly child material.

It was Klein's view that early relations with the individual's primary objects, shaped by projection and introjection, form a major part of the individual's inner world, and that these relationships emerge in all relationships with other people, especially in the relationship with his analyst. She says:

> The relationship to the psycho-analyst at times bears, even in adults, very childlike features, such as over-dependence and the need to be guided, together with quite irrational distrust. It is part of the technique of the psycho-analyst to deduce the past from these manifestations.
>
> (Klein 1959: 243)

In Chapter 2, 'The emergence of early object relations in the psychoanalytic setting', Irma Brenman Pick shows in differing contexts the emergence of early object relationships within the analysis, sometimes covert and subtle and sometimes occurring as violent eruptions. She explores the way in which patients relate to their objects, both defensively withdrawing as well as more openly facing them. She discusses how the way in which the analyst is seen by the patient contributes to the analyst's understanding of the patient's object relationships. Central for her is the question: 'Who is the analyst for the patient at any particular moment?' Her examples from child and adult patients are from all ranges of disturbance: a mute, retarded, and autistic child on the one hand to adult patients who in many respects function well but, in the subtleties of their relationships to the analyst, clearly show primitive object relationships.

Klein's early work was highly innovative in its uncovering of new types of material through her play technique with children, and it was evident that she was already developing ideas of her own such as the earlier dating of the superego and the Oedipus complex, but from 1919 until 1935 her fundamental underlying theory, her model of the mind and of psychic development, was basically similar to that of Freud and Abraham. In particular, she followed Abraham's notion of phases of the libido (Abraham 1924). In 1935, however, she published a paper entitled 'A contribution to the psychogenesis of manic-depressive states', which marked out her ideas as having a new element of theory. In this paper she propounded the view that the infant passes through a process of realizing that the objects he has loved and those he has hated are actually one and the same person; part-objects come to be recognized as whole objects (not breast only but mother as a whole); the infant becomes aware of concern for the object, feels guilt over the psychic attacks he has made on his object, and ardently wishes to repair the damage. The anxiety concerning damage and loss Klein called 'depressive anxiety' and she outlined the characteristic defences used against it. Klein thought that this constellation of anxieties, defences, and object relations began in the second quarter of the infant's first year, but she called this development the 'depressive position', not the 'depressive phase', in order to emphasize her conviction that the individual does not simply pass through this phase and leave it behind as a fixation point. Throughout life, she thought, there is a constant to-and-fro towards and away from the anxieties and defences of the depressive position (Klein 1935; 1940). As time has gone on Klein's followers have made very full use of her concept of the depressive position, though they have become less concerned than was Klein herself about the precise dating of its onset in infancy.

In Chapter 3, 'The Oedipus situation and the depressive position', Ronald Britton takes Freud's 'nuclear complex', the Oedipus complex, and shows how Klein links it with her own concept of the depressive position, sometimes described as her most important contribution to psychoanalysis. Further, he describes the history and development of the depressive position and the Oedipus complex and shows how they are completely interdependent. The capacity to relinquish sole possession of one parent and the acceptance of the reality of the parental couple, that is, the prerequisite for working through the Oedipus complex, is dependent on achieving the tasks of the depressive position; namely, the acceptance of the separate existence of the object and the consequent emotions of envy and jealousy that this precipitates. To accept the separateness of the object is to accept implicitly the reality of the object's other relationships, especially relationships between the parents. Britton discusses the defences against such acceptance. He gives a number of detailed clinical examples from his work with adults and children.

After the storm caused by Klein's conception of the depressive position and the interchanges of the Controversial Discussions in the early 1940s, Klein produced yet another fundamentally new view in 1946 in a paper entitled 'Notes on some schizoid mechanisms'. In this paper she describes the 'paranoid–schizoid position' with its character-istic persecutory anxieties of threat to the individual (as distinct from the threat to the object, the anxiety characteristic of the depressive position). She describes the defences typical of the paranoid–schizoid position, especially splitting of the object into good and bad with corresponding splitting of the ego into good and bad, accompanied by phantasies of projecting parts of the ego (and/or aspects of internal objects) into the object; these phantasies of projection are accompanied by identification of the external object with the projected aspects of the ego or of the internal object (projective identification); the other defences she describes as omnipotence, idealization, and denial. She stresses too that phantasies of projection and introjection interact from the beginning of life to build up the inner world of self and objects. Once again, although she describes the paranoid–schizoid position as characteristic of earliest infancy, she does not think of it as a phase. Throughout life, in her view, there is a constant fluctuation between the paranoid–schizoid and the depressive positions.

In Chapter 4, 'The equilibrium between the paranoid–schizoid and the depressive positions', John Steiner describes the two basic positions and the different defences against anxiety that exist in each. He then goes on to describe the equilibrium between the two positions, empha-sizing that in her choice of the term 'position' Klein was distinguishing her position from Freud's and Abraham's notion of 'stages' or 'phases'. He makes use of Bion's chemical notation PS ←———→D to denote the dynamic nature of the equilibrium. Steiner continues the chapter by showing that in his view there are further subdivisions within each position. In the paranoid–schizoid position there is a continuum between normal splitting necessary for healthy development and pathological fragmentation leading to formation of 'bizarre objects' (Bion 1957), which is associated with more serious disturbances in later life. Within the depressive position there is a state dominated by *fear of loss of the object* which can be associated with denial of psychic reality, and a state in which the *loss of the object can be experienced*, leading to an enrichment of the personality. These states within the depressive position are closely linked to work on mourning, and Steiner discusses mourning in some detail, considering Freud's work on mourning and that of Klein and the relationship of mourning to the depressive position. Appropriate clinical illustrations are given to show these different types of mental organization.

As described above, Klein put forward the idea of projective identification in the course of discussing the paranoid-schizoid position. To her it was not an especially central idea, but it has been discussed and written about more than any of her other concepts. In Chapter 5, 'Clinical experiences of projective identification', Elizabeth Bott Spillius describes Klein's concept of projective identification and the developments and refinements of it, especially by Bion and Joseph. In so doing she describes three ways in which the idea of projective identification is now used by Kleinian (and other) analysts, especially in Britain. Klein's original description focuses on projective identification as an unconscious phantasy which influences the way the patient perceives the analyst. Bion focuses, in addition, on the way the patient's actions may sometimes induce the analyst to feel what the patient often unconsciously wants him to feel. Joseph's extension of Bion's usage examines the way the patient constantly but unconsciously 'nudges' the analyst to act out in accordance with the patient's internal situation. Spillius emphasizes the way in which these more recent developments focus on the constant and continuing interaction between patient and analyst. She also makes the point that clinically she sees little benefit in attempts to assert that one model is the 'correct' one, and, further, little clinical benefit in attempts to distinguish projection from projective identification; she believes that all three models are valid ways of looking at clinical material and that all three are likely to be used by the same analyst at different times, sometimes within the same session.

Michael Feldman's discussion in Chapter 6, 'Splitting and projective identification', overlaps considerably with that of Chapter 5. (The lectures were given on separate Lecture Days.) Feldman discusses Klein's theory of projective identification and early splitting, emphasizing the accompanying split in the ego as well as the splitting and projection of internal objects. Not all projections are of bad parts of the self. The self may rid itself of good parts, a process which, if excessive, may result in over-dependence on the external object. Feldman gives detailed clinical illustrations in order to explain the process of projective identification and describes three fragments of analyses with patients. The first shows how the patient quickly projects a confused and humiliated part of himself into the analyst; in this case the patient was able to recover that part of himself in response to an interpretation. The second patient manifests another important and more recently

7

described aspect of projective identification – the provoking of the analyst to re-enact early object relationships which, if interpreted rather than enacted, allows the possibility of modifying the original state. The third case was one in which the analyst was forced into action whatever he did. Feldman shows in this way how Melanie Klein's theory of projective identification, modified especially by the work of Bion, Rosenfeld, and Joseph, is used centrally in clinical work today.

It will be evident from these six chapters that later Kleinian analysts, especially Segal, Bion, Rosenfeld, and Joseph, have developed and in some cases altered Klein's original formulations, but that these formulations remain a basic source of inspiration (Spillius (ed.) 1988).

Klein's last major work was her book *Envy and Gratitude* in 1957, again a work that aroused considerable controversy but has been found valuable by her followers, particularly Bion, whose work forms the subject matter of the last three chapters of this book.

A definitive biography and/or critique of Bion's work has not yet been published. His autobiography, *The Long Week-End* (1985), gives a highly idiosyncratic account of his early life, schooling, and traumatic and heroic experiences as a tank commander in the First World War. Partial accounts of his work have been given by Meltzer (1978), Grinberg *et al.* (1975), Williams (1983), and Grotstein (1981b).

He was born in 1897 in Muttra, India, where his father was an engineer and administrator. India made a lasting impression on him, and amongst the writings that he often used in his work was included the *Bhagavadgita*. He was parted from his family at the young age of eight to attend school in England, as was the sad custom at that time. During the First World War he joined the Royal Tank Corps and saw a great deal of action, for which he received two high awards for gallantry, though in his later book, *A Memoir of the Future* (1975), he makes it clear that in the chaos and fear of war, what happens is very confused and unclear and is re-written and falsified afterwards in an attempt to find sense where there is none. These experiences clearly influenced him deeply and one constantly sees them reflected in his psychoanalytic writings, especially on psychotic states. He went to Oxford where he excelled in sport and graduated in Modern History. After a brief period of teaching, and already interested in psycho-analysis, he went to University College Hospital to study medicine in order to pursue a career in psychoanalysis. One of his appointments was with Wilfred Trotter, a surgeon with a deep interest in psychology who was known for his book on groups, *The Instincts of the Herd in Peace and War*, upon which Bion clearly drew in his work on groups.

After qualifying he went straight into psychiatry and was soon working at the Tavistock Clinic, and started analysis with John

Rickman. His psychoanalytic training was interrupted by the Second World War, during which time he was very active in using and developing his ideas on groups in the treatment of psychological casualties as well as in the selection of officers, and this early work with groups formed the subject of his first paper (Bion 1943). After the war he completed his psychoanalytic training in analysis with Melanie Klein, which had a profound influence on his development as an analyst.

His radical work on groups arising out of his war work and at the Tavistock Clinic (Bion 1961) gave way to more purely psychoanalytic study from the 1950s onwards. Along with a number of other Kleinian analysts at that time, notably Herbert Rosenfeld and Hanna Segal, he analysed many psychotic and borderline patients, drawing especially on Melanie Klein's paper 'Notes on some schizoid mechanisms' (1946). This work formed the basis for several important papers, especially 'The differentiation of the psychotic from the non-psychotic personalities' (1957), 'On arrogance' (1958), 'Attacks on linking' (1959), and 'A theory of thinking' (1962a). Bion's ideas on psychosis are difficult to characterize as belonging to either of the classifications of psychoanalytic theories of psychosis sometimes known as the 'defence' theory and the 'deficit' theory, and described in more detail by London (1973) as the 'Unitary' theory (see especially Arlow and Brenner 1969) and the 'Specific' theory (Katan 1979; Frosch 1983; Yorke, Wiseberg, and Freeman 1989; see also Grotstein 1977). Like the 'Unitary' theorists, Bion tries to develop an overall model of thinking that encompasses neurosis as well as psychosis; but he also emphasizes that individuals who, whether for constitutional or environmental reasons, persistently cannot tolerate frustration evacuate frustration and bad experience, which leads to their being unable to develop capacities for rudimentary thought, so that they are in a psychic state similar to that described by adherents of the 'Specific' school as a fundamental deficit in mental representation.

Bion was a prominent member of the British Society during the 1950s and 1960s and was President from 1962 to 1965. During the 1960s he drew together much of his previous work, most notably starting with *Learning from Experience* (1962b), then *Elements of Psychoanalysis* (1963), *Transformations* (1965), and *Attention and Interpretation* (1970); all these books developed the ideas put forward in 'A theory of thinking'. In 1968 he retired from active membership of the British Society and went to live in Los Angeles where he continued to write, practise, teach, and to develop his ideas until he returned to England in 1979 shortly before his sudden illness and death later that year.

Bion's work has had a profound influence on the clinical practice of all Kleinian psychoanalysts in the British Society as well as many belonging to the Independent and Contemporary Freudian groups. Many analysts who are not especially conversant with Bion's work are none the less using his ideas in the way they apply Klein's ideas to their work. It is often more difficult for those not brought up in this analytic tradition to understand Bion's writings fully, not least because he tries to write about emotional experiences which do not easily lend themselves to description in words.

Much of the clinical work described in this book, as well as some of the ideas in the chapters on Klein, have been influenced by Bion. Thus the use of the notation PS ←——→D and the way it conveys the dynamic nature of the relationship between paranoid-schizoid and depressive positions, described by Steiner in Chapter 4, arises from Bion's development of Klein. The way that Spillius describes changes in the use of the term 'projective identification' since Klein, and the way it has often come to include a consideration of the counter-transference, arises from Bion's concept of the 'container' and the 'contained' (Bion 1962b), which is discussed in detail in Chapter 8 by Britton. The three chapters on Bion that follow are not intended to 'cover' Bion in any complete way, but rather to help readers see how British psychoanalysts of a Kleinian tradition try to use his ideas clinically.

As discussed above, Bion's early formative psychoanalytic work was with borderline and frankly psychotic patients, and it was at this time that his ideas of the nature of the psychotic personality were delineated, especially in his 1957 paper 'The differentiation of the psychotic from the non-psychotic personalities'. In Chapter 7, 'Psychosis: not thinking in a bizarre world', Edna O'Shaughnessy discusses this, showing how Freud's idea of the 'pleasure principle' is used in an object-relations framework. A personality that is intent on warding off pain and frustration mobilizes a phantasy that not only the bad experience is projected into the object but also that part of the mind that can register the experience is similarly felt to be got rid of. If this method of dealing with experience persists, the psyche cannot develop an apparatus – an ego – that is capable of doing anything other than ridding itself of bad experiences, which results in the loss of reality sense; this constant projection of bad experiences leads to the building up of a psychic world of terrifying persecutory objects which the self takes more and more drastic measures to protect itself from. She describes how Bion emphasizes the fundamental difference between the conception of the world by the psychotic and the non-psychotic individual or parts of the personality; namely, that psychotic functioning is dominated by fragmentation and the expulsion of the *means* of knowing reality – the senses, consciousness, thinking – that is, the very means of protecting the mind from psychosis. She discusses Bion's necessary preconditions for the development of psychosis as both constitutional and environmental, and emphasizes that even the best of mothers, although alleviating the situation, may also provoke envy of her capacity to cope and so lead to a distorted and disturbed relationship in any case. The primary object of the psychotic individual is likely to be seen as not nurturing at all, but to be a type of greedy, vagina-like breast which denudes communications of meaning. The treatment of psychotic patients is clearly, therefore, an enormous and difficult task, but O'Shaughnessy emphasizes that Bion felt that, provided they attended therapy or analysis, such patients were treatable, though the objectives were in many ways different from those of neurotic patients. The analysis oscillates between movement towards an aberrant depressive position and movement towards an aberrant paranoid-schizoid position, but with gradual development of a capacity for more humanized contact with the object. O'Shaughnessy illustrates this by material from two patients in whom the psychotic parts of the personality were dominant.

The expulsion of the means of knowing reality contrasts markedly with the other tendency, which Bion sees as being present very early indeed, not only to love ('L') or hate ('H') the object but also to *know* it and *be known* by it ('K'). It is this basic human tendency to know and be known that leads to attempts to tolerate frustration. Such tolerance leads to *not* using projective identification to get rid of frustration but, on the contrary, leads to *holding on to an experience of having a 'No Breast'*, as Bion often calls it, which is a rudimentary 'thought'. In Chapter 8, 'Keeping things in mind', Britton shows how, in Bion's model of thinking, the capacity to endure the absent object, the 'No Breast', can only come about if the baby first experiences (and can tolerate experiencing) an object that can allow projection; that is, an object that can be hated or stirred up in various ways but can hold on to these experiences long enough to be able to respond to the baby in a way that gives the baby an experience of some of his bad, projected feelings being modified by the mother. If the mother can provide this, and if the baby is able to feel 'contained' by the experience, he can eventually introject this function as well as the mother's particular response. This is what Bion calls 'alpha function', the essential ingredient of the rudimentary thinking mind. Indeed Britton illustrates vividly the consequences of not having such an object in infancy.

Bion's ideas of containment and non-containment contribute greatly to the analyst's view of what is going on in an analytic session, since arising out of this is the notion of projective identification as a primitive but quite normal method of communication between baby and mother and in analysis between analysand and analyst. Finally, Britton discusses Bion's ideas of the possible ways in which failure of containment can come about. Like O'Shaughnessy, Britton notes Bion's stress on both constitution and environment. With psychotic patients he thinks there is almost certainly a constitutional factor manifesting itself as envy of the mother's containing functions, but he concludes that in many cases the infant has experienced an unresponsive object who cannot be sensitive to the infant's projections. Britton adds some of his own ideas about the effects of the father for good or ill on this situation.

The notion that the wish to 'know' one's object is a fundamental drive is taken further by Ruth Riesenberg Malcolm in Chapter 9, 'As if: the phenomenon of not learning', in which she draws especially on Bion's ideas on thinking and learning. Bion speaks of *knowing* ('K') as the defining link between self and object, but, just as an envious relationship to the object can change a loving link to a hating one, so an envious relationship to an object around *knowing* may change a wish to know into a wish not to know, from 'K' to what Bion calls 'minus K'. The primary object where minus K is dominant is experienced not as a mother or breast that wishes to know and understand the baby's state of mind, but as an object that denudes the baby's experience of meaning. In such a psychic world the infant, and if it persists, the adult, will be unable to learn from experience, as Riesenberg Malcolm shows in her clinical illustrations of several patients who invested all their energies in keeping analysis in a static condition. She further introduces and discusses a type of defensive splitting which she calls 'slicing', distinguishing it from fragmentation.

Bion's writing is very much influenced by his ideas on the nature of language, and he tries to modify his communication with the reader in various ways which make the actual experience of reading much of his work a difficult and often unnerving one. His frequent use of algebraic notation − 'PS' for paranoid-schizoid, 'D' for depressive, 'K' for knowing, 'beta elements' for undigested experience, 'alpha function' for rudimentary thought − is designed, he says, to avoid conveying unwanted associations and sensuous communication. Whether this is useful or not is perhaps debatable, but it is very much his style of writing and that is what readers are faced with if they wish to understand his work. It is hoped that this brief look at his ideas through the clinical work of three present-day analysts will help the reader at least to see that many analysts find his discoveries very useful in their work.

To conclude: this book attempts to describe some of Klein's and Bion's basic ideas and to show how they are used and are being developed in everyday clinical work by several analysts. Many of Klein's and Bion's ideas have not been discussed, and many recent developments have been passed over, but I hope that the present selection will whet the reader's appetite.

Child analysis and the concept of unconscious phantasy

PATRICIA DANIEL

Introduction

In this chapter I shall focus on the first phase of Melanie Klein's work, roughly between 1919 and 1934, when she was working within the theoretical framework of Freud and Abraham and before she made her own theoretical formulations. During this period there were two major developments: the working out of her play technique for child analysis, a clinical development, and a broadening of Freud's concept of unconscious phantasy, a theoretical development. These two developments were closely linked, as so often happens in psychoanalysis.

Melanie Klein's contributions to psychoanalysis are rooted in her work with children. From the beginning she was convinced that full Freudian analysis of young children was possible and, as Hanna Segal (1979) describes it, Klein's stroke of genius was to realize that play is the child's natural means of dramatizing his phantasies and working through his conflicts. I shall describe her play technique and try to show how it gave her access to the liveliness of the projective and introjective phantasies operating in the mind of the very young child. Freud and Abraham had started to conceptualize the introjects; that is, the parts and aspects of persons taken into and active within the mind as unconscious phantasies. Her play technique, like a new tool, made it possible for her to build on their work and to show the importance for psychic development of the nature of these introjects. Her understanding of the operation of unconscious phantasies in young children's minds opened up the liveliness and richness of the internal world of objects. These discoveries eventually led her and her co-workers to deepen and widen the concept of unconscious phantasy and to formulate ideas about how the infant's psychic world is gradually built up

14

from birth onwards. I shall include illustrations of the operation of infantile phantasies as they emerge in the analysis of children and adults.

Discovery of the psychoanalytic play technique

Apart from 'Little Hans' whose analysis was carried out by his father under Freud's (1909) direction, it is generally thought that Dr Hildi Hug-Hellmuth was the first to attempt psychoanalytical work with children. She also taught and must have influenced Anna Freud, who came to child analysis with a background in teaching. At that time both Hug-Hellmuth and Anna Freud worked only with children of latency age between six and twelve whose verbal associations were limited and sporadic, and at first they tried to deal with this difficulty by playing with the child and seeing it in its family circle so as to get to know its everyday life and relationships. These early pioneers of child analysis sometimes analysed their own children as well as those of friends and colleagues, probably not yet fully realizing the power of the transference in a child.

An important step in the development of Klein's play technique came with the analysis of her youngest patient Rita, aged two years and nine months. Rita had night terrors, was inhibited in her play, and suffered from excessive guilt and anxiety. Since analysis of so young a child was a new venture, Klein (1955) approached the task with some trepidation, and her misgivings seemed to be confirmed in the first session when she was left alone with Rita in her nursery. Rita was silent and anxious, and asked to go out into the garden. So out they went, Rita seeming less frightened when they were in the open. While in the garden Klein interpreted Rita's negative transference to her, telling Rita that she was afraid of what Klein might do to her and linked it to her night terrors. After these interpretations Rita's fear lessened and she was able to return to the nursery and play. It was during this analysis that Klein concluded that the transference situation could only be properly established and maintained if the child feels that the room, the toys, and the whole analysis are separate from his ordinary home life. So she provided her next patient, another little girl, with a box of small toys to be used only by her during analytical sessions.

By 1923 her principles of child analysis and her technique were worked out.

Melanie Klein held that the child's play expresses its preoccupations, conflicts and phantasies, and her technique consisted in analysing the play exactly as one analyses dreams and free associations, interpreting phantasies, conflicts and defences. The child's drawings and his associations to them are often particularly instructive.

(Segal 1979: 42)

The room, the toys, and the analyst provide the setting for the play technique. Klein favoured very small toys, as they are easy for little children to handle. Nowadays when we see very disturbed children in analysis small toys are also safer when hurled about. As far as possible they should be nondescript so as not to suggest games. The choice of toys is important because the child's free play functions like free association in the analysis of adults. They usually include bricks, a few animal and human figures in two sizes for use as adult and child figures, a few small cars and trucks, a few small balls and containers; also paper, pencils, and crayons, glue, scissors, string, and plasticine. If running water is not available, then a jug of water and a bowl are provided. The purpose of these materials is to provide the child with maximum scope for his imaginative play. The room has a table, at least two chairs, and a couch. The furniture is arranged so that the child is free to express aggression without danger to himself or undue damage to his surroundings. Each child has his or her sessions at fixed times, fifty minutes five times a week.

There is an interesting illustration of Klein's technique which is more fully described in Volume 2 of *The Writings of Melanie Klein*, Chapter 2, entitled 'The technique of early analysis' (1932: 17). Peter, aged three years and nine months, was timid, difficult to manage, unable to tolerate frustrations and inhibited in his play. He had a younger brother. His analysis was intended to be a prophylactic measure. At the start of the first session Peter puts the toy carriages and cars first one behind the other, then side by side and then alternates this arrangement. In between whiles two horse-drawn carriages are made to bump into each other so the horses' feet are knocked together, and Peter says, 'I've got a new little brother called Fritz.' Klein does not enquire about the little brother, the external reality; she pursues the internal reality, for she asks 'What are the carriages doing?' He replies, 'That's not nice,' stops their bumping but soon resumes it. Then he knocks two toy horses together in the same way. Klein makes her first interpretation; she says, 'Look here, the horses are two people bumping together.' Peter says, 'No, that's not nice,' but then he says, 'Yes, that's two people bumping together and now they are going to sleep.' He covers them with bricks, and says, 'Now they're quite dead; I've buried them.' In the second session he repeats this sequence with cars, carts, carriages, and two engines. Then new material emerges. He puts two swings side by side, shows Klein the inner long part that hangs down and swings and says to her, 'Look how it dangles and bumps.' Then comes her interpretation. She points to the dangling swings, the engines, carriages, and horses, and says that they are each two people, 'Daddy and Mummy bumping their thingummies.' Her practice was to find out beforehand from the parents the child's own words for genitals, faeces, urine, and bodily functions. First Peter objects, 'No, that isn't nice,' but he continues knocking the carts together, and soon after he says, '*That's* how they bumped their thingummies together.' Then he speaks about his little brother again. In the rest of the second session Peter's play develops to reveal more details of his phantasy of his parents' intercourse, his own wish to join in, and he and his brother masturbating together. As Klein follows him and interprets, so Peter shows her more.

Through her analytic work with young children, some seriously ill, Klein became convinced that the child forms a transference and that his play is symbolic of unconscious phantasy and equivalent to free association in adults. Therefore she thought that the sole function of the analyst is to interpret the unconscious phantasies and conflicts as fully as possible from all that the child patient does and says, as in adult analysis. These remain the principles underlying the Kleinian approach to child analysis today, and many of these have become more or less generally accepted in British psychoanalytic child analysis. But in the 1920s these were revolutionary ideas and aroused controversy in the psychoanalytic societies. Technical differences were linked to differences in theoretical approach. Anna Freud (1927) and her followers held that a child could not develop a transference neurosis while still emotionally dependent on its parents; they also thought the child's ego and superego were too immature to establish a full analytic process, so the analyst should adopt, they suggested, a supportive role to guide the ego and strengthen the superego. At this time Anna Freud also thought valuable work with children was done only in a positive transference and the negative transference should be avoided.

On the other hand Klein had found the rich, imaginative world of unconscious phantasy, peopled with internal objects, which suffused the young child's mind. These internal objects were distinct from the actual parental objects, although in interaction with and influenced by them. It was, for Klein, this world of inner phantasy objects which was alive and active, which determined the transference and which could then be modified by interpretation. In contrast to Anna Freud at that time, Klein found that the primitive superego was extremely harsh and cruel, but she also found that its strength could be reduced by interpretations, particularly of the underlying anxiety and guilt.

In her early papers on child analysis she gives a wealth of detailed description of children's play and verbal associations and the simple direct way in which she couched her interpretations. What is so striking is the acuteness of her observations and her clinical insights which enabled her to grasp the meaning of the unconscious phantasies unfolding in the play and to trace the transference within them. Above all she was sensitive to the anxieties of her little patients and aimed to direct her interpretations to the point of maximum anxiety because she found that the resolution of anxiety brought progress in analysis and in the child's development. She observed, listened to, and took seriously the anxieties of very little children, as Freud had done with adults suffering from mental illness. In the 1920s and 30s her discoveries opened up a whole new area in the understanding of children.

In child analysis the aim is to try to understand and interpret the dimension of unconscious phantasy, which Klein had discovered is always present in the ordinary play of a child. I want to give you a straightforward clinical example of very ordinary child material, where the little patient is not doing anything dramatic. She is playing in an ordinary sort of way. This is an obsessional girl of six who has been in analysis for a few years; she has one sibling, a sister fifteen months older than herself. In the second session after a summer holiday break she spends the first part sitting back rigidly in an armchair in a corner of the room. She remains silent and watchful, and occasionally her eyes flick rapidly round the room. Gradually her glances are directed more often to me, to the chest of drawers, and to her open drawer there. She gives no sign of hearing me when I talk to her about her being so scared of me and the room, though she wants to look around, how she feels she needs to control herself and me so that nothing frightening or unexpected can happen. Eventually she edges her way cautiously to her drawer where she rummages for a good ten minutes, apparently looking for all the loose bricks scattered amongst the jumble there. She places all the bricks on the table and two bags containing wooden figures and wooden animals. She checks their contents and then checks the bricks, returning to the drawer to hunt for more. She finds two tiny ones and puts some crumpled-up drawings she had done the previous term into the wastepaper basket. Next she groups all 24 bricks into their various shapes and colours and places them in their bag. She returns the other two bags to her drawer. She checks the time by her large watch and empties all the bricks onto the table; for a minute or two she seems very uncertain. Then she places four square bricks to form a square and later puts a thin blue stick brick inside the square; as I am uncertain as to what she has done I move nearer to see better, and she dismantles it. Next she builds a low wall of bricks, and on her side of the wall and attached to it is a flat square with a small coloured brick inside the square. On my side of the wall but separate from it she builds a pillar of bricks with coloured, rounded ones at its top. She surveys both structures and glances at me, expecting an interpretation. She has not spoken.

As she is obsessional, her initial defence against her anxiety in being with me again is to check and control both of us. The interpretation of her fear reduces the anxiety and then some detail of her unconscious phantasy gradually emerges in her behaviour and play. I think it is something like this. Her first anxiety is whether something has been taken from her, while she has been thrown out during the holiday like the crumpled drawings she put in the wastepaper basket. The next anxiety is what has been going on in the room and inside me, symbolized by the squares of bricks, in her absence. Is there a baby? Are there blue bricks in the square? She isn't certain, as I am uncertain and moves nearer to look, but she suspects there are. I think the pillar outside the wall represents the penis which she suspects got inside and produced a baby, but which she now believes is somewhere outside. Klein was the first to realize the unconscious drama contained within such simple ordinary behaviour and play, and to appreciate the richness and power of these infantile phantasies in the minds of children and adults.

The internal world

It has often been said that Freud discovered the repressed child in the adult and Klein discovered the repressed infant in the child. She saw how children and adults are dominated by their unconscious phantasied relation to parts of their parents, like breast or penis, introjected during the oral phase in infancy and already repressed in young children. These relations to parts and to whole people fill the child's unconscious mind and have personal characteristics and personalities, for they can be seen as loving, appreciative, hating, greedy, or envious and so on. Klein thought that from the beginning of life the infant, in phantasy, introjects his mother's breast and repeatedly splits its good and bad aspects with the aim of introjecting the good ones and projecting and annihilating the bad ones. In the Kleinian view it is of fundamental importance that the infant, and in analysis the patient, gradually internalizes a predominantly benign picture of his mother, or analyst, since this forms the basis for all loving, lasting reparative relationships in the future. This benign process can be seen at work in a little girl of two who was struggling with her first separation from her

19

parents. She spent much of the morning of the third day clutching her teddy, staring out of the window, looking for her parents in the street beyond. She became more miserable and then felt physically sick, so she agreed, with some relief, to go to bed. As she wearily climbed the stairs pulling teddy after her she was heard consoling him: 'Poor Teddy, he's so sick; poor, poor teddy.' Her miserable self was projected into teddy but there was also a kindly, caring internal mother who was sympathetic and with whom the little girl identified.

Through her work with many young children Klein discovered the primitive Oedipal situation and the origins of the superego in a new world of the child's complex phantasies and anxieties about his mother's body. Phantasies include ones that mother's body is full of good things, such as milk, food, magic faeces, babies, and father's penis, which is imagined as incorporated by mother during intercourse, at first believed to be oral. In phantasy this body and its riches are desired, attacked, and robbed, and sometimes the destructive, envious attacks are motivated more by hatred than desire. There are also phantasies of repairing and restoring mother's body. Klein thought that the basic persecutory anxieties in children and adults originated in the oral and anal phases of development and in this primitive relation to the mother's body which was imagined as containing father's penis. Later, when father is beginning to be seen more as a separate person, the baby's phantasy creates what Klein called the combined parental figure. For she found her small patients produced play material which showed both parents in intercourse combined into one figure. While such a picture helps the baby to deny the pleasure it imagines its parents receive from each other, none the less the envy and jealousy are projected onto this combined figure. This is the basis of children's nightmares of many-headed or many-legged monsters. The intensity of the baby's anxieties in relation to the mother's body are similar in intensity to those found in adult psychotic patients. These anxieties are also the driving force in the displacement of interest from the mother's body to the world around and push the baby toward developing an interest in the external world.

The concept of unconscious phantasy

Klein's early work led on to a reformulation of the concept of unconscious phantasy. Her notion of unconscious phantasy comes from her view of symbol formation as the link between unconscious phantasy and reality. By symbolizing in words or play, the child expresses and modifies his phantasies through his experience of reality.

All a child's activities, and those of adults too, even those most geared to external reality, also express and contain their phantasies. External reality affects our phantasies, and our phantasies influence our perceptions of external reality. She and her co-workers focused their analytic work on locating and interpreting the content of unconscious phantasies and the unconscious functioning of the ego, and this led them to a wider view of phantasy. They came to the view that the primary contents of all mental processes are unconscious phantasies and that these phantasies form the basis of all unconscious and conscious thought processes (Isaacs 1952). Juliet Mitchell (1986) has this to say about Klein's concept of phantasy:

> phantasy emanates from within and imagines what is without, it offers an unconscious commentary on instinctual life and links feelings to objects and creates a new amalgam: the world of imagination. Through its ability to phantasize, the baby tests out, primitively 'thinks' about its experiences of inside and outside. External reality can gradually affect and modify the crude hypothesis phantasy sets up. Phantasy is both the activity and its products.
>
> (Mitchell 1986)

My brief account of Klein's first two sessions with three-year-old Peter and the material from the six-year-old girl did, I hope, illustrate the way in which children use toys and play to symbolize their phantasies. I now want to give an example from an adult analysis when an infantile Oedipal phantasy of interrupting parental intercourse and taking the place of one or other parent dominated the patient's mind and external experiences during a weekend and subsequent Monday session. My account is limited because my aim is to show the patient's relation to her infantile phantasy.

She is a severely ill young woman with a delusional quality to her external relationships and in the transference. She suffered very early deprivations, and reacts over-hungrily. She is unmarried and has a sister and a brother, two and three years younger than she. This patient had intended to miss a Friday and a Monday session as she had time off from her job and she was going to stay with her parents who were staying in the country. She missed the Friday session but arrived a few minutes early for the Monday one. She begins by saying she feels awful having come without ringing to let me know, only on the way here did she think she should have rung me first. After a pause she thinks I am annoyed because I haven't said anything yet; she feels she's barged in and shouldn't have come. She really ought to have let me know and now she is sure I am furious with her. When she was in the waiting room she imagined a friend of mine had just popped in and we were talking when she (the patient) had interrupted us. The atmosphere is now rather awkward and gradually a sense of mystery develops. She hints at why she returned to London, implies she had had a bad time, being blamed for all that had gone wrong at the weekend, but she hasn't yet told me what actually happened and what went wrong. After we explore this, she describes how she discovered her favourite dress had been taken by her sister, who intended to wear it and left it hanging up in her own room. Furious, the patient snatched it back and gave it to a friend who happened to be visiting, so her sister could not get it back. Then she was blamed by her father for not having left the house keys out for mother who was arriving late at night. The patient had driven off with the keys, needing them herself. By now she is distressed and becoming confused as to who was blaming and jealous and evil and hated. When we sorted some of this out she then explained she was feeling so unhappy she decided to return to London on Sunday evening. Instead of returning to her own flat she spent the night in the family home, to comfort herself. But she was further upset to find her sister there with her boyfriend, so the patient ended up sleeping in her parents' bedroom in her mother's bed. She emphasizes that her parents dislike anyone else sleeping in their bedroom and mother hates anyone except the patient sleeping in her bed.

My view of this is that the weekend separation stirred an infantile phantasy of being shut out from the pleasure of parental intercourse going on in the country, as she was from the analytic intercourse.

Her fears of losing her place and her valued possessions are symbolized by the favourite garment and her session, both of which she gives away in retaliation. She becomes increasingly consumed with jealousy and hatred, locks out me (on the Friday) and her mother (on the Saturday night) and takes the penis herself, symbolized by the keys. But then she feels guilty and blamed by an angry father/superego/me. Becoming more desperate and miserable, she ousts father and gets inside mother herself, symbolized by her bed, and later back into the Monday session and onto the couch.

Thus the full force of the primitive impulses and desires expressed in her unconscious phantasy influenced the patient's actions over several days in her external life, and in her analysis, and her conscious feelings and perceptions of people were distorted by it.

By establishing the pervasive existence and operation of unconscious phantasy Klein laid the groundwork for more radical modifications of psychoanalytic understanding which followed. The much earlier origin of Oedipal phantasies led to the reformulation and re-dating of the Oedipal situation, and the evidence of the very small child's persecutory superego led to the realization that the superego, too, had much earlier roots in the infantile mind. These findings adumbrate her later formulations of the paranoid-schizoid and the depressive positions. All these insights emerge from her early grasp of the ubiquitous, fundamental nature and operation of unconscious phantasy and of the internal world established by it in each of us.

2

The emergence of early object relations in the psychoanalytic setting

IRMA BRENMAN PICK

We are all familiar with the notion that the way we look at people will affect what we see; it is, after all, part of common parlance that we may look at someone with adoring eyes, through rose-coloured spectacles, or with hate, with a mote in the eye, with black looks or dirty looks or even with looks that kill, and that these feelings may affect or even grossly distort the accuracy of our perceptions, as well as the way we react to others. This in turn may affect their actual behaviour towards us.

Indeed, our receptors – eyes, ears, mouth, nose, and touch – all that with which we take in from outside, are parts of our living and evolving selves. And if we speak of black looks or dirty looks, we imply that the look is putting something nasty into that which is looked at. Because we project so much – and then take in – we are not sure how much of what we are perceiving is really there, and what has been added to, either with love or hate, of what comes from ourselves. We receive experiences, and also in phantasy or reality express or expel feelings and parts of ourselves, good and bad, as well as our own internalized history.

Of central importance in Melanie Klein's work was the emphasis she placed on the idea that these forces were operative from the very beginning of life. She postulated that even the very young infant, responding in a loving way to the internal breast that comforts and supports and feeds him, also attributes his own loving feelings to that breast, and takes in bit by bit and stores experiences of a loving and comforting mother: this is based in part on taking in real nourishment and real experience from the breast, but it is also coloured by what he attributes (and contributes) to it. Conversely, frustrated and in a rage, he attributes cruel feelings and motives to the breast, and 'perceives' it as hurtful and attacking.

Implicit and essential to an understanding of Klein's views of the unconscious are the ideas discussed in detail by Susan Isaacs in 'The nature and function of phantasy' (1952) – that the mind is a whole. The higher parts of the mind do not act independently; the unconscious is not merely a vestigial or rudimentary part of the mind. It is the active organ (perhaps we might say the font) in which mental processes function. No mental activity can take place without its operation, although much modification of its primary activities normally ensues before it determines thought and behaviour in an adult. The original primary mental activity has been called unconscious phantasy. There is no impulse, no instinctual urge which is not experienced as unconscious phantasy. Even if a conscious thought and act are completely rational and appropriate, unconscious phantasy underlies them.

Because of the intensity of their own early or primitive feelings, infants build up inside, initially, two separate types of picture of what we call the primary object – one ideal and the other horrendous. One might say that infants see the world in black and white, their perceptions of the outside world much distorted by the intensity of their own moods, needs, and impulses. Infants build up an internal world, initially peopled by internal figures or objects, experienced as all good or all bad – the view of the world Klein described as the paranoid-schizoid position. With development, the infant gradually begins to learn, with pain, that it is the same mother whom he hates and attacks and fears, whom he also loves and values and by whom he is supported – this being described by Klein as a move to the depressive position.

In the psychoanalytic setting we have the opportunity to observe and study these processes as they emerge in the relationship with the analyst. Freud's great discovery that feelings and impulses were transferred from earlier relationships, not remembered but re-lived and re-experienced in the relationship with the analyst – the transference – was also applied by Klein in the field of child analysis.

In this chapter I want to present some clinical material, not to prove the existence of these forces, but rather to illustrate how we, as Kleinian analysts, might try to understand them. I shall start with material which is rather stark in its portrayal of these early processes and then move on to more evolved material in which, although much modification of the primary activities has ensued, as Susan Isaacs described, I believe we can trace back the earlier determinants of thought and behaviour, the emergence of the early object relations.

Maxi is a prematurely born, grossly disturbed and retarded seven-year-old. In his first session (his mother was present) he was apparently unseeing of the analyst, but focused on the light hanging in the centre of the room. The mother explained that he wanted the light on; he pushed it, making it swing, and then cowered in a corner watching it, at first frightened and then with an ecstatic gaze.

The analyst interpreted that the light was all the world to him, that he wanted it to shut everything else out, and to take it as something very good into himself. Following this intervention he picked up a work basket which he tried to attach to the light, and then started to make clear sucking movements with his mouth and asked for water.

We note that the child apparently does not notice the analyst and focuses on the light; yet he quickly communicates a wish for something to be switched on, makes it move, and then becomes frightened of it. I would suggest that, terrified in the new world of the consulting room, the child desperately searches out and finds something to cling to – the light, a light which soon becomes connected with his physical thirst (the breast itself). We see both his cowering and his ecstatic gaze. For him it is no ordinary light, but at one moment a terrifying object, at another, a wondrous one.

The analyst conveys acceptance – switching on the light and putting into her words her understanding of his feelings. Maxi then attached the work basket to the light and made sucking movements with his mouth; it seems to me that the analyst had stimulated his wish to communicate and his thirst; was he also thirsting to communicate about his earliest experience of being in an incubator with only a light to cling to? The analyst responding to his request left the room to fetch him water, Maxi took a sip and then angrily interrupted the session.

The next day Maxi went straight for the light, began swinging it and asked for water; this time the analyst interpreted that he had made a link to her (as 'Dottoressa Acqua') which he wished should be continuous. Following this he indicated that he wanted her to swing the light with her head whilst he alternatively and simultaneously did so with his hand.

Even in this very retarded child, as in the young infant, in Klein's view, we see evidence of mental activity, linking, recognizing, holding in his mind a continuity from one session to the next. There is an organization which recognizes and stores memories of the past, and part of what it stores is the relationship with another person in however rudimentary a form. Maxi now communicates that he wants something from the analyst's head, which is felt to be good and which he wishes to link with his hand movements. I should think there is a complex movement – eyes/face/head – and the idea perhaps that the food for thought comes from the analyst's head (mind) and that this is what he thirsts for. He then tries to incorporate this mental functioning into being an attribute of the light which he can move with his hand;

something akin to the small infant holding or touching the breast, a movement which may express both his loving co-operation with the feeding breast as well as his wish to believe that it is totally under his control or even part of himself.

So we see him poised between the possibilities of the beginnings of a building up of a human relationship and a wanting to attach to a mechanical object (like the light) that he feels to be under his control, just as we saw him breaking off the possibility of a relationship with the analyst in the previous session when he felt interrupted or misunderstood, or even a combination of the two.

Of course we would be interested to understand more, by following the vicissitudes in the development of his relationship with his analyst, about what interactions may have taken place between his own propensities and the circumstances of his life that have resulted in his relationship being so heavily weighted in the direction of depending on mechanical objects rather than human intervention, but that might be the subject of another discussion.

Gradually the healthy infant begins to differentiate what belongs to himself and what belongs outside himself; whether he cowers because of threats of danger from outside or because he fears the violence of his own feelings and his perceptions of something approaching reality. But the primitive – that is, the early parts of the self, and of the early objects, idealized or hated – remains with us and affects our perceptions.

We are all at times taken over by such states of mind; maturity is about being able to re-view these issues, knowing what distorted pre-views we may form. Neal Ascherson, in an article in the *Observer* some years ago, commenced an article with a story of a woman pursued by a hostile assailant; she ran desperately for cover; finally, from behind the safety of her own front door, she demanded: 'What do you think you are doing?', to which he replied, 'What do you think *you* are doing? It's your dream, not mine.' Ascherson was alluding to the pictures which East and West formed of each other.

We see things partly accurately, partly coloured by emotions, and partly by the relationships we made in the past. I am focusing on the way in which an interaction of the past is re-enacted in the present. A patient, Mr A. (who had had an appalling childhood history), had been very provoking with requests for time changes; now he asked for a change for what seemed to be seriously considered reasons. For what seemed to me to be equally legitimate reasons, I said that I would see if it was possible and give him an answer the following day. We all know what it's like to be kept waiting for an answer in this way – and there is a question as to whether I was unconsciously vengeful or autocratic in the way I arranged this.

The next day he was extremely 'prickly', made no mention of the time issue, and told me a dream from which I report only this fragment. In the dream a couple of Japanese soldiers associated by him to torturers, but also to me – my consulting room is in an area flanked by Japanese schools etc – are flying overhead in a helicopter, dangling a baby or a very young child from the air above a war zone. He is appalled that they should expose a baby to this horror.

When I interpreted his belief that I was keeping him dangling as a kind of retributive torture in what he felt to be a war about times, he agreed. The interesting quality of his reaction, the refusal to mention it again, the bottling up of grievance, all seem to suggest a bitter relationship with an earlier object. So whilst on the surface we might appear to be having an ordinary transaction about times, at another level he believes that either I am being kept dangling by a couple of torturing 'soldiers', or he believes himself to be in a relationship with a couple in power who engage in brutal and sadistic cruelty in dominating and tyrannizing over infantile needs. His parents placed him in care when he was a very young boy; he has grounds for such a view of the 'couple'; he himself also engages in such behaviour. In addition there is evidence of a patient who selectively clings to the excitement of such atrocities to avoid the ordinary everyday pains of life, including having to bear uncertainty (waiting) and the fact of there being a couple (the parents) so that his needs are not the only ones to be considered.

When this patient perceives 'the couple', this couple is experienced not as getting together to nurture him, nor even that he has to bear feelings of being excluded when they come together in their own intercourse, but that they come together to torture the baby. This would correspond, I think, to Klein's view of the very early Oedipal anxieties (1928; 1945). She considered that very early on there were precursors to the Oedipus complex, and that one of the phantasies of the infant was of combined parents imbued with dangerous propensities as a result of the infant's projections.

One might say that the couple dangling the baby in this cruel way, in his dream, is his unconscious phantasy of what I do with my partner when I keep my patient waiting. Let us consider that in part he correctly perceives me as an analyst engaged in autocratic or tyrannical vengeance. None the less, I believe there is evidence of a pattern (of which this is an example) of the way he negotiates 'ordinary' arrangements with his wife at home, or with me, that leads me to believe that what we are dealing with is an established vicious circle in which he feels entrapped with such torturing and tortured objects and that this torturing overrides whatever the current reality might be.

I shall now try, at more length, to describe the emergence of early object relations in a session in the analysis of a thirty-year-old woman. Married, with two children, she has the internal resources to function well in many areas of her life. Yet she presented for analysis with hypochondriacal anxieties, intense, frenzied anxiety states, and a quite severe depression. She feels both considerably helped by her analysis and intensely grateful, whilst at the same time there is a more hidden excitement in which she is contemptuous of me, mocking and triumphant in the face of my short-comings.

On the Friday before a long weekend she reports a dream; she explains that before the dream the telephone had rung late at night. It was her husband's firm in Israel. (Things are going very badly there and they may be forced to return because of not being able to finance remaining here.) But she decided to turn over and go to sleep.

In the dream they are at first in what seems like a railway station; there are gate exits on either side and many pillars (she pronounces the word as if it were 'pillows') supporting the structure. From there they take a sailing-boat; the sea is extremely beautiful – that wonderful clear marine green – and there are many little red fish (as on the Coral Beach in Eilat). They are with the children; suddenly a spurt of something very black – oil – comes up from the sea; not with an oil platform or anything, a spontaneous eruption. But they go on until they are suddenly threatened with being taken over by an enormous wave and she awakens in a state of anxiety.

She immediately embarks on a very long account of a boat outing some years ago when she was in the last stage of pregnancy with her younger child. An unpleasant, bossy co-owner of the boat stayed out swimming too long. When they tried finally to return, it was getting dark, there was no wind, the engine failed; they hailed another boat whose owner agreed to tow them but this boat had no lights and did not know the way.

By now, she continues, everyone on both boats was quite hysterical. When they used their radio to contact the control tower all they were told was that there was no help available.

Although she was talking of a no-response to a cry for help, she continued talking. I noted that she kept me out and seemed to be comforting (and exciting) herself with her talk. This is a good opportunity to raise the question: what sort of object am I for her, and what sort of anxiety was she escaping from? I wondered what she was turning away from (as when she 'switched off' from the phone call last night) when she returns to a familiar old story; I asked about the railway station with the two exits that was left behind. She immediately associated to the Holocaust (her parents' families were almost all wiped out) and began sobbing bitterly. I thought that the coming long weekend with the underlying threat of losing the analysis altogether felt like a horrendous deportation, in which she was threatened with feeling wiped out.

This is complex material – evolving through many and diverse dimensions of time and space; the precipitating disturbing phone call from which she withdraws; an earlier traumatic event related to giving birth; the Holocaust, and so on. But I want to look specifically at the expression of early object relations in this material.

The patient tries to turn away from the alarm she feels about being dropped and left; whilst there is an underlying panic of a horrendous magnitude about deportation, she feels triumphant in turning her back on this (and on her husband's need for support) and takes a trip inside a dream (and in the session inside a familiar story) in which she believes that she 'sees' with exquisite clarity. But the black slick erupts – spontaneously – and then comes the wave of – rage? panic? In the story which she associates to the dream there is a growing realization of not having the necessary equipment; the wind, the engines, the necessary illumination, or capacity to find the way; and there is a realization of needing help. But whom to turn to for help? I think the co-owner of the boat may represent in part herself, but may also be a picture of a father felt to be preoccupied with his rules or his pleasures (swimming inside *mother*?). The other boat may represent parental figures who in principle are felt to be willing to help but are so taken over by their own wave of grief and panic (the Holocaust) that they cannot see where they are going either. She feels that the message is that no help is available. This is her picture not only of the actual parents but also of her internal objects; that is, of what is now available to her internally to help her cope with anxiety. There may be some reality to this picture of her parents.

But if we study what happens we see that the issues are a little more complicated. For example, she despises her husband for becoming so anxious, yet effectively gives him a message that no help is available from her to share these anxieties. Recently she had seen me chairing a public meeting and became excitedly triumphant when she believed me to be in difficulties in it; and I think now fears that I will be unable or unwilling to help her. In the session she is in part co-operative; for example, she brings her dreams and associations, and in part I think wants to flood me with a wave of material such that I will be in the dark, unable to see what is going on, and in a frenzy about not being able to cope, whilst she presents with this initial picture of herself in full sail (pregnant) and seeing beautifully.

I think that part of what erupts spontaneously (albeit without a platform – breasts) is a considerable envious rivalry with a mother/analyst in the chair experienced as able to cope when she cannot, and in part it is hatred and vengeance against parents/analyst experienced as not coping. And behind that she has a kind of black despair about whether the object on whom she depends, who is asked (like the other boat) to carry her and lead her to safety, will be overwhelmed, in the same plight as she is. This triumph over her objects, since they are the very objects upon whom she depends for survival, also represents a cruel triumph over her own needs. She turns to me, as a mother, fears losing me, and triumphs over me at the same time.

The hallmark of Klein's contribution was to show how these problems exist not only in relation to the Oedipal couple, but that these splittings occur in relation to the primary object from very, very early on in life. In the transference we see a patient who creates an idealized object and wants to put the analyst in that position (a ship in full sail 'seeing' with exquisite clarity), but, being idealized, such an object is of no real value; or she creates a denigrated object of no real value. So there is no full realization that it is the same mother analyst who looks after her who also leaves her, no real object to help her deal with life.

Returning to the patient's dream we also note that there are pillars/pillows supporting the structure – representing I think both the solidity and firmness and the vulnerability of the supporting objects. Thus, she recognizes that there are objects which support her and upon which she depends for support, but she also makes more grandiose assertions when she is carried away by the wave of her own infantile omnipotence. In the dream she turns to an idealized object with which she is fused; she is *in* the sea/see, seeing with exquisite clarity. When this breaks down in the face of the obtrusion of a wave of reality, this object relationship is exposed as having no substance. We have much experience in the analysis of a repeated turning to such idealized objects, turning her back on the objects that give her cause for worry, including the worry of having to take on board a full awareness of her dependency; in the process she turns her back on the object that is available to support her.

She turns to me but also wants to triumph over me in what Herbert Rosenfeld (1964) has described as a narcissistic object relationship, she sees herself as superior to the real breast; like the superior 'Aryans' she triumphs over overwhelmed, worried 'Jews'. In that situation she finds it necessary to turn her back on seeing her object as damaged, but she also fears the object, now experienced as a superego who will

31

overwhelm her with a wave of retributive hatred, and she shows only contempt for her vulnerability and her plight, and the message is that no help is available.

I wish to describe a final example from a child patient who presents a drawing very similar to my previous patient's dream. Jack, a restricted, withdrawn eight-year-old, presented himself to his therapist as distanced and remote, and projected into her very painful feelings of being worthless and unwanted, whilst he behaved as though he could give her all sorts of material if he so wished. There was ample evidence of projective identification in which he seemed to have grown very big, to have taken over the function of a rather distanced mother, and to have left in her his feelings of being small and needy.

In the sixth week of his treatment, his therapist told him about her impending holiday. He appeared to be unruffled and drew a picture of an idyllic country scene in which all was peaceful. This seemed to coincide with his apparently peaceful reaction to the news of her coming holiday (akin to my patient's lovely sea). Material began to emerge, however, which indicated that he imagined that they would be on this idyllic holiday together; the holiday was experienced not as an interruption or loss but an ideal fusion. Following interpretation that he was defending against anger about the coming separation, he referred to the grassy tufts in his drawing and said they might be bombs, then anxiously contradicted this saying, 'It really is grass.'

Shortly afterwards when the analyst reminded him of her holiday dates, he responded in an apparently sophisticated way: 'I know you're going to America [she is American] and that you'll be with a man going to a restaurant.' Then he painted another picture, again beginning with an idyllic country scene, but now there was a boat departing (the analyst) and in the sea was an enormous whale with very large teeth and a huge menacing tail erupting into the landscape. It seemed that behind the apparently bland acceptance of the coming holiday something huge was erupting which was disturbing the peace. This whale with its biting teeth and menacing tail seemed to open up big issues that needed to be dealt with. In a still later session he produced a map of America in which the 'holiday' boat was arriving. The continent was, however, surrounded by menacing whales and sharks, filled with snakes described by him variously as a lake of death, a blood forest, a volcano representing, I think, dangerous faecal and urinary excrement. His own internal volcano seemed to be erupting. However, while these drawings were vivid, he himself seemed to remain cut off. It gradually emerged that he was seeing himself as a gifted artist whose drawings he felt were much in demand. In this way he felt that his artistic productions were more significant than the therapist's interpretations.

He ended a very elaborate and beautifully presented story (written by him when the therapist was away ill for a couple of days) with this conclusion: 'The starfish is called a starfish because it is shaped like a star. It is poisonous and could kill anybody.' He acknowledged no interpretation, but later told his father that he believed his therapist would die in the holidays. We see that the wish to be loved, to be the special and star child, the narcissistic defence against the experience of loss, becomes compounded by more poisonous, lethal feelings.

Like my adult patient, he fuses with an idealized object, and in the process feels bereft of a good and strong object than can be relied upon to survive and to support him to deal with the 'volcanic' eruption of his own hatred and anxiety in the face of loss.

Summary

I have tried to show in different contexts and in child and adult patients the emergence of the early object relationships; sometimes this is covert and subtle, sometimes more like a violent eruption.

We see in these patients the great need they have for a good internal object, an object they can rely on that will help them to contain the anxieties, bear the vicissitudes of life, sustain them with the strength to encounter new difficulties and to enjoy the challenges of life.

In fact, as Bion remarked, the first thing a patient does when he finds an object who does provide the support is to tell the object what it was like not to have it. We see Maxi dependent on mechanical objects; a patient clinging to the excitement of coupling for purposes of torture; a patient fused with an idealized object whilst escaping the horror of facing damage and of a retributive superego or conscience.

From a technical point of view, my main emphasis is on the question: who is the analyst at times of need, or indeed who is the analyst when he addresses the patient with an interpretation? For if the analyst is experienced as the patient's internal object he may not be experienced as much help; instead he may be felt to be a mechanical purveyor of 'acqua' or interpretations, a sadistic torturer, an idealized figure, or a broken-down or retributive person. But we do see in the patients I have described, even in Maxi, the search for an object that will understand and give support and we see too the great impulse to find an object with whom the patient can communicate and who will provide nourishment and help. It was part of Melanie Klein's considerable contribution to elaborate the details of the dynamics of these very early processes, of what Freud called the dim and shadowy area of the mind.

3

The Oedipus situation and the depressive position

RONALD BRITTON

An earlier version of this chapter was read in Vienna in 1985 and published in the *Sigmund Freud House Bulletin*, vol. 9, no. 1, 1985.

I find it a sobering thought that in a few years' time a century will have passed since Freud first put pen to paper to describe what now we so often refer to as the Oedipus complex.

In May 1897, in a letter to his friend Wilhelm Fliess, he wrote that he now thought that an 'integral constituent of neuroses' was hostile impulses against parents (Freud 1897a: 255). 'This death wish is directed in sons against their father and in daughters against their mother.' He wrote a succinct further note: 'A maidservant makes a transference from this by wishing her mistress to die so that her master can marry her (cf. Lisl's dream about Martha and me) ' Lisl was the Freuds' nursery-maid and she had reported a dream of her mistress having died and the Professor marrying her. Five months later, in October, Freud described in a further letter his discovery of this same configuration in himself in the course of his own self-analysis. This persuaded him that such wishes might be ubiquitous. And he conjured up a universal audience for the Greek drama of *Oedipus Rex*, in which 'Each member was once, in germ and in phantasy, just such an Oedipus.' Freud refers to the horror generated in the audience by 'the dream fulfilment here transplanted into reality' (Freud 1897b: 265) — the horror, that is, of Oedipus killing his father and marrying his mother, leading Jocasta his mother to suicide and Oedipus to blinding himself. However, whether it is the royal court of Thebes or Lisl in the nursery, we notice in the two different sexes the same elements:

a parental couple (symbolic in Lisl's case);
a death wish towards the parent of the same sex;

a wish-fulfilling dream or myth of taking the place of one parent and marrying the other.

The Oedipus complex has remained at the centre of psychoanalysis ever since, and is the daily currency of our work in various forms. For some years Freud referred to it as the Nuclear Complex.

What substantial additions have been made to our knowledge about it since Freud? I consider that the most significant new additions to our perspective on this were made by Melanie Klein, partly in her clinical observations of Oedipal manifestations in very small children, partly in her papers on the Oedipus complex (1928; 1945), and indirectly by her concept of the depressive position (1935; 1940). Donald Winnicott considered that her most important contribution to psychoanalysis was the concept of the depressive position, which he wrote 'ranks with Freud's concept of the Oedipus complex' in the development of analysis (Winnicott 1962: 176).

In this chapter I want to describe some of what she added to the understanding of the Oedipus situation, what is meant by the depressive position, and how in my view the introduction of this concept necessarily changes our understanding of the resolution of the Oedipus complex. As I see it these two situations are inextricably intertwined in such a way that one cannot be resolved without the other: we resolve the Oedipus complex by working through the depressive position and the depressive position by working through the Oedipus complex.

Though Freud referred to Oedipus Rex, as I described, in 1897, he did not use the term 'Oedipus complex' in a paper until 'A special type of object-choice made by men' in 1910. In this paper he puts it that the boy who begins to desire his mother anew and hate his father as a rival 'comes, as we say, under the dominance of the Oedipus complex'. Under this dominance he emphasizes another element which is made even more central by Melanie Klein. In Freud's words, 'He does not forgive his mother having granted the favour of sexual intercourse not to himself but to his father, and he regards it as an act of unfaithfulness' (Freud 1910: 171).

The parents' sexual relationship is centre stage in this account and is at war with the child's exclusive relationship with his mother. The child's awareness of the parents' relationship is conspicuous in Freud's various accounts of the Oedipus complex during this period, culminating in his account of the 'primal scene' as the centrepiece of his case study usually known as the 'Wolf Man' (Freud 1918). This study was based on analytic work done between 1910 and 1914; it was written in 1914 but not published until 1918 (Editor's Introduction to Freud

1918). Freud began during that analysis to speculate on 'primal phantasies', an archaic inheritance of innate ideas, one variety of which would be some sort of primitive precursor of the primal scene (Editor's footnote to *Moses and Monotheism*, Freud 1939: 102). Such innate ideas, were they universal, would predispose us all to construct some version of parental intercourse fleshed out by experience and imagination (Freud 1916: 367–71). This notion would seem to be a forerunner of Bion's theory of preconceptions (Bion 1962b: 91). After 1916, however, the primal scene plays a less conspicuous part in Freud's account of childhood sexuality. In such of his writings as 'The infantile genital organization: an interpolation into the theory of sexuality' (1923b), 'The dissolution of the Oedipus complex' (1924a), and 'Some psychical consequences of the anatomical distinction between the sexes' (1925), it is displaced as a central concern by the castration complex and penis envy. However, his preoccupation with primal phantasies including the primal scene is once more to the fore in his late works such as *Moses and Monotheism* (1939: 78–9) and *An Outline of Psycho-Analysis* (1940: 187–9). But Freud never incorporated the primal scene and its associated phantasies as a principal component of the Oedipus complex. In contrast to this, Klein not only did so but made it central in her account of what she called the 'Oedipus situation' (Klein 1928; 1945).

Klein was to find ample confirmation of Freud's primal phantasies in the analyses of young children. She also found that such phantasies occurred very early, and that in very young children were violent, terrifying, and bizarre. She also found that, in conjunction with the aggressive phantasies of children against parental intercourse and mother's body containing unborn babies, there was guilt and despair at the damage done in phantasy and there was a wish to repair the damage. Where this reparative wish failed, the damage was denied and magically restored by omnipotent manic reparation. When this belief failed, obsessional methods were resorted to, with compulsive acts of symbolic significance carried out in desperate efforts to undo what had been done in imagination.

In Klein's view the Oedipal situation began in infancy and underwent a complex development occupying years before reaching its zenith at the age of four. This was the age of what has come to be called the classical Oedipus complex as described by Freud. Klein also emphasized that the development of our attitude to knowledge (the epistemophilic impulse – or the urge to know) is considerably influenced by these early experiences of the Oedipus situation. She described what enormous hatred could be stimulated by the child's feeling of ignorance in the face of the irreducible mysteries of parental sexuality and how in some children an inhibition of all desire for learning could follow. In one of her earliest papers, in 1926, she wrote:

> At a very early age children become acquainted with reality through the deprivations which it imposes on them. They defend themselves against reality by repudiating it. The fundamental thing, however, and the criterion of all later capacity for adaptation to reality, is the degree in which they are able to tolerate the deprivations that result from the Oedipus situation.
>
> (Klein 1926: 128–9)

What are these deprivations? Why are they so crucial that they influence our hold on reality and therefore our sanity? We are better equipped to consider these questions in the light of the notion of the depressive position, a concept Klein first formulated a decade later (1935; 1940). In Klein's view the phenomena of the depressive position, which begin to develop between three and six months and continue thereafter, involve major steps forward in psychic integration. Part objects (breast, face, voice, hands, and so on) are recognized to be parts of one single, whole object. Love and hate, instead of being experienced towards separate objects, are realized to be directed towards the same object. The infant begins to feel guilt over his attacks on the good object and becomes afraid of the damage done to it and afraid of losing the object; he has a strong wish to make reparation to the object he believes he has damaged. Klein points out the simultaneity of the depressive position and the Oedipus complex. 'The early stages of the Oedipus complex and the depressive position', she says, 'are clearly linked and develop simultaneously' (Klein 1952b: 110). Or again:

> Jealousy is based on the suspicion of and rivalry with the father, who is accused of having taken away the mother's breast and the mother. This rivalry marks the early stages of the direct and inverted Oedipus complex, which normally arises concurrently with the depressive position in the second quarter of the first year.
>
> (Klein 1957: 196)

If the integration of the depressive position fails, the individual cannot progress fully towards developing a capacity for symbol formation and rational thought. One of several possible abnormal outcomes is that the individual may resort to obsessional, compulsive acts to put right the imagined damage.

I found such obsessional efforts underlay the activities of a middle-aged patient of mine whose phantasies of parental intercourse were of sadistic violence, containing as they did not only her perceptions of her father as a brutal robber taking away her mother, but also her own projected cruel vengeful wishes against her mother for betraying her. Whenever images related to these early phantasies would come to mind she would take desperate remedies to rid herself of what she called these 'bad thoughts'. She would repeatedly try to flush them down the toilet; wash them out of her hair; and empty them down the garbage-disposal chute.

In order to understand why this took such a concrete form, and required physical acts, it is necessary to realize that in some people the development of symbolic capacity is not fully achieved. Klein linked the development of the capacity to symbolize to the working through of the fundamental anxieties she had described, but it was Hanna Segal who was in later years to show that the capacity to symbolize, and therefore to make symbolic, mental reparation was a consequence of working through the depressive position (Segal 1957).

I propose now to leap forward in time in order to discuss how I see these ideas in the 1990s. I see the depressive position and the Oedipus situation as never finished but as having to be re-worked in each new life situation, at each stage of development, and with each major addition to experience or knowledge. As we know, the effect of new knowledge in the scientific world which transcends our pre-existing view of things is at first disrupting: it needs investigation, abandonment of some existing order, and its integration demands modification of our world view. It arouses our hostility, threatens our security, challenges our claims to omniscience, reveals our ignorance and sense of helplessness, and releases our latent hatred of all things new or foreign: all things, that is, that we do not regard as some extension of ourselves, or as encompassed by the familiar boundaries of our mental landscape. In these moments we are once again in the same state as the infant in the depressive position as described by Klein. The depressive position arises inevitably and naturally in infancy as a consequence of the developing capacities of the child: to perceive, to recognize, to remember, to locate, and to anticipate experience. This is not simply an enlargement of awareness and knowledge, but the disruption of the existing psychic world of the infant. What had previously been separate worlds of timeless bliss in one ideal universe of experience, and terror and persecution in another alternative universe, now turn out to be one world. And they come, these contrasting experiences, from one source. The fount of all goodness, loved in phantasy as an ideal breast, turns out to be the same object as the hated bad breast previously perceived as the source of all things bad and the essence of evil. Innocence is lost, then, in its two senses. We are no longer innocent of knowledge – having eaten of the fruit of the tree of knowledge we can no longer live in Eden. And we have lost our innocence in the sense of becoming capable of guilt – guilt because we now know we hate that which we love and which we regard as good.

The depressive position, like the Oedipus complex, is an extremely rich and many-faceted concept, and long before its discovery in psychoanalysis it had been explored in theology and in literature. In English literature, it is perhaps most notably explored in Milton's *Paradise Lost*, and I think most beautifully expressed in Wordsworth's ode, 'Intimations of immortality from recollections of early childhood'. In this he recounts poetically the struggle at the heart of the depressive position, the struggle not to reject the banal goodness of ordinary life when contrasted with the hints of a lost ideal world. As he puts it, to 'find strength in what remains behind' when 'Nothing can bring back the hour/Of splendour in the grass, of glory in the flower' (Wordsworth 1804: 302).

As I have said, the depressive position is provoked by, and establishes, that greater knowledge of the object which includes awareness of its continuity of existence in time and space and also therefore of the other relationships of the object implied by that realization. The Oedipus situation exemplifies that knowledge. Hence the depressive position cannot be worked through without working through the Oedipus complex, and vice versa. Freud made clear that repression of the complex intact was a foundation for neurosis; that something else was needed, which he called its dissolution, for healthy development. Something had to be given up (Freud 1924a). In 'Mourning and melancholia' (1917) Freud linked the preservation of sanity and reality to the relinquishment of the idea of the permanent possession of the love object. But he did not apply this to the dissolution of the Oedipus complex.

Following Freud's ideas in 'Mourning and melancholia', Klein linked giving something up in the external world, as we do in weaning, for example, with the process of mourning. This is a process which necessitates once again that we give up the expectation of finding an ideal world which might be realized in the material world, and that we recognize the distinction between aspiration and expectation, the distinction between the psychic and the material. She saw this as a process of repeatedly anticipating something and then discovering it to be absent. She considered it to be a means of relinquishing the object in the material world and simultaneously installing it in the psychic, or inner, world (Klein 1935; 1940). In Bion's language, a preconception which is followed by a negative realization gives a thought if the frustration can be borne that it does not give a thing (Bion 1962b). If the frustration cannot be tolerated, the negative realization (that is, the absence of something) is perceived as the presence of something bad – 'a bad thing' – with the notion that it can be got rid of; hence the phantasy that a state of deprivation can be eliminated by abolishing things. If, because of this failure to transform preconception into idea, there is in phantasy an incorporation literally and concretely of the external object into the inner world, then a state of mind exists which underlies some psychotic and severe obsessional states. For example, a patient of mine, prior to seeking psychiatric help, had sought the removal of something bad inside her, which made her have bad thoughts, by surgery.

An essential element in the depressive position is the growth of the sense of distinction between self and object and between the real and the ideal object. Hanna Segal has suggested that it is a failure to make such distinctions that results in a failure of symbolization and the production of 'symbolic equations' – that is, symbolic objects experienced as identical with the original object (Segal 1957).

A similar state of affairs is implicit in Freud's account of the neurotic patient's treatment of all subsequent love relations as if they were with the original Oedipal object. Just as in the depressive position the idea of the permanent possession has to be given up, so in confronting the parental relationship the ideal of one's sole possession of the desired parent has to be relinquished. The Oedipal phantasy may become an effort to reinstate it, to deny the reality of the parental sexual relationship. If this denial threatens to sever the individual's hold on reality, then the Oedipal romance may be preserved, by splitting it off into an area of thinking protected from reality and preserved, as Freud described, like Indians in a reservation (Freud 1924b). This reservation, which may be an area of day-dream or masturbatory fantasy, can become the place where some people spend most of their lives, in which case their external relationships are only used to enact these dramas to give a spurious claim of reality to their fantasies which lack 'psychic reality'. In other people the reservation may be preserved as an island of activity, such as a perversion, separated from the mainstream of the individual's life.

I am making a distinction here claiming some phantasies possess psychic reality, not by their correspondence with an external reality, but by the sense of 'truth', which Bion (1962a: 119) has suggested is a similar quality in relation to our inner world as a sense of reality is in relation to the external world. He proposes that a sense of reality comes from our combining data derived from different sensory modalities, such as sight, hearing, touch, and so on – 'common sense'. In a similar way he suggests that a sense of truth comes from our combining different emotional views of the same object. Thus, when we acknowledge we hate what we feel to be the same person as someone we love, we feel ourselves to be truthful and our relationship to be substantial. If this recognition of ambivalence is evaded by, for example, using the Oedipal configuration to perpetuate our divided universe by having one permanently good parent and one permanently bad, then this reliable sense of the truth of things is lacking, and this, I think, often leads to repetitious patterns of behaviour designed to assert a reality that lacks inner conviction; for example, to repeated re-enactments of stereotyped Oedipal situations in life.

If, in order to achieve the integration described by Bion, the common view of the object has to be established and tolerated, it means that the mother perceived as a feeding and loving mother has to be perceived as the same person as the sexual mother – that is, in the first instance as father's sexual partner. This poses great difficulty for many people. It often seems to be represented by pictures of women as degenerating or deteriorating, or, as in a male patient of mine, scarred. He recently began an affair with a romantically idealized woman and he described with lyrical intensity the meal they recently had together which was flawed only by her mentioning her former husband at the end of the meal. Then something began to go wrong for him, and, when he saw a small scar like a flaw on her leg, he became impotent and subsequently could not bring himself to contact her. Having cut himself off from her, he then developed a state of alarm about her, convinced she must be severely depressed and possibly suicidal. I was familiar with this pattern in this patient and it manifested itself in the transference recurrently. What seemed to happen was that his aversion to the thought of parental sexuality was represented by the image of a disgusting woman, and the hostility provoked by his envy and jealousy led him to 'cutting himself off', an act which he felt mutilated those he subjected to it. The anxieties which ensued about the fate of the woman are typical of those Klein designated as depressive anxieties.

This sort of reaction was a relatively recent development in this patient. When he first came into analysis, women were either pure and remote, or the objects of pornographic study and perverse scoptophilia as excitingly degraded figures. He had also suffered paranoid anxieties intermittently and had secret states of grandeur and elation when he assumed the characteristics in his mind, by projective identification, of a magical, omnipotent father. In essence he was predominantly in the state that Klein describes as the paranoid-schizoid position (see especially Chapter 3) and the more recent phenomena I have described represented a partial move towards the depressive position.

The perception of parental sexuality in the paranoid-schizoid position is phantastic and often horrific. It may form the basis of

41

psychotic anxieties and perverse practices or crimes. One notable example is the phantasy of the combined parent figure. The figures are formed by the projection of the infant's oral, anal, and genital desires into the parental intercourse, which is perceived as perpetual; this results in phantasies of conjoined figures such as mother with father's penis or father inside; or father with mother's breasts or mother inside him. In some patients the recognition of parental intercourse may be regarded as destructive of everything good about mother, or breast, and hence destructive of the good internal object which would be equated with everything good in the world. Thus in such a patient the primal scene is likely to be seen as a catastrophe leading to a fallen world. As in the myth of the Garden of Eden, it is eating the fruit of the tree of knowledge which brings the Fall: the advent of shame and sex, and the avenging angel.

In such patients there may develop a hatred of knowledge and sometimes quite literally hatred of seeing or of being seen. If enlightenment is experienced in a persecutory mode it is felt to be forced in, not taken in. Then either the whole personality is protected from knowledge, or, by splitting, part of it may be. This was the case in a patient who, in response to an interpretation of mine which suggested that as a result of her experience she might see things differently, said, 'Seeing and thinking have nothing to do with feeling and dreaming!'

In this patient, who would be described as a severely borderline psychotic case, that aspect of herself which privately she called 'me' was kept from the light of ordinary day and from any interaction. It remained infantile, blind, hardly differentiated, and persecuted by any light. Until analysis, where it emerged in a psychotic transference, this aspect of her had remained undisclosed, unmodified, and ungratified except by a variety of autoerotic activities. For a long time in analysis this aspect became manifest in my room only in the dark underneath a blanket on the floor, where she could feel the carpet, or, tentatively, my shoe. She was terrified at such times because she was allowing contact with me and therefore access to me, and felt that I might force enlightenment into her as a sort of psychic rape.

Exploration of these phantasies which she feared so much eventually became possible. They existed in her mind, of course, but initially she believed them to be externally located and likely to come from me. When they emerged they were of horrific and confused images of a sort of part-object sexuality – mouths with fierce teeth biting off penises; breasts with holes where nipples should be; strange representations of female genitalia with penises in them; the inside of a maternal body like a cave with corpses in it.

I am not describing here the gradual emergence into the light of repressed thoughts and desires but the efforts of someone to defend themselves from what they perceive as substantial assaults; perceived as actual, not symbolic, and external, not internal. The patient in the paranoid-schizoid position has buried his unacknowledged thoughts in others, or in his actions, or in his perceptions. And though they are symbolic in form they are treated as things. Analysis in such cases, as Betty Joseph has pointed out, is likely to be a scene for action rather than thought, and it is the analyst's task to reclaim for thought what may otherwise be dispersed in action and reaction (Joseph 1978).

As the individual moves more towards the depressive position, the sense of persecution is diminished and the theme of loss is more to the fore. A boy of nine, Peter, whom I treated, was reacting to what he experienced as a reactivation of loss in the Oedipal situation. His only sibling, Carol, was fourteen years older than Peter and had recently married and was now having a baby. Peter was doing badly at school as he spent most of his day in a dream. The content of these day-dreams I was to discover in the course of his treatment. They were extremely elaborate stories which he illustrated in fine details or modelled in Plasticine. Their purpose was to provide him with that 'reservation', which Freud referred to, where he could reinstate old phantasies of omnipotent self-sufficiency based on his body. His favourite stories were about a primitive tribe he had invented which he called the 'Wallies'. They had a mine with many underground levels and a central shaft. The chief Wally sat at the top of the shaft and was fed on the food which was mined from the mud and brought up from below. He also received jewels from the mine. Peter confided that he thought of his body as like the mine with little men inside. Later in his treatment he said that though the Wallies said they were jewels that they found in the mud, really they were germs. In this elaborate fantasy Peter reinstated an old phantasy of feeding himself from his own faecal products as he now fed his mind on his own ideas and tried to ignore his teacher's words and mine; it was an effort to turn from the painful conflicts he experienced in any dependent relationship.

The issues involved in this were illustrated in his first session following a holiday break after a year of treatment. He had begun to react to my leaving him and this was portrayed in his play. He began to draw the Wallies who were preparing to resist the attempt of Baron von Wally to invade their territory. Baron von Wally was a character who had emerged to become the leader of the Wallies since Peter had been in treatment. Now, however, the Wallies had got rid of him for not feeding them, and when they had fought him off they returned to their mine. When I talked to Peter about his feelings of my having deserted him like the Baron and his turning away from me angrily as a result, he began to play with two rulers on the table. Then he said they were two ships, one British and one American. I felt there was some transference reference in this as my woman colleague, who saw Peter's parents regularly, was American, a fact he had always been conscious of. The two rulers in his game bumped their ends together and Peter said that when the two ships came together a little pug dog who was swimming in the water was crushed in between them.

This I think portrayed Peter's experience of two ruling parents coming together and of his finding it to be a crushing blow. He responded to my interpretation along these lines by taking up the camel from among the animals. The camel had two humps and on top of each a sort of protruding harness. Peter said this was a nipple and began to feed the little animals from it. Then he looked at the two humps intently and put his finger on them. When his finger came to the space between them he shuddered and said, 'Ugh – I don't like that bit in between; it makes me feel funny.' I linked this to his not liking gaps between sessions and that it reminded him of what it would be like between feeds. Peter said, 'Daniel, my baby, drinks from a cup.' This was said defiantly, and he added, 'He used to drink from my sister's tits but he did not like it so after about three weeks he gave it up, so now he drinks from a cup.' He looked at me very intently and then said, 'I think it was after one week.' My break had been for three weeks.

When in the course of time Peter's reaction was not to turn away but to express his anger more directly, it also became clearer that he was worried about the effects of his anger on his parental objects, both in the transference and at home. His father's health and his mother's anxious nature lent some substance to this; but it was also clear that Peter was unwilling to give up the omnipotence that led to such depressive anxieties. When he began to do so in the transference, he became assailed by a new thought that I was going to start treating a new boy. Peter hated to think he did not know things, and so was apt to assert that if he suspected something it was true. So it was with the new boy, whom he declared was going to come from his class at school. This intolerance of ignorance was linked to his feelings about exclusion from some parts of his parents' life, and now he faced it again with his sister's marriage, pregnancy, and childbirth.

Peter was not such an envious child as my borderline patient. Nor had he such disturbed parents; and he had not therefore restricted his own capacity to see in the way that she had, and he was able to take from me in a way that she was not able to for a long time. His own body-based system of self-feeding and self-production represented by the Wallies' mine was a rivalrous organization to the parents' feeding and reproducing capacity, and was prompted by his envy of their knowledge and their creative ability. It was mitigated, however, by feelings of love and appreciation: initially he tried to protect both by putting them alongside each other; that is, his narcissistic dream-life and his relationships with his family existed in parallel.

When she first wrote about the depressive position Klein felt that the issue which decided whether we could move forward through it, or remain defended against it and vulnerable to the development of psychotic depressions, was the balance between hate and love. If we believed that our good feelings and therefore our good objects could survive integration with our bad feelings and bad objects, we could move forward. I think the combination of the depressive position and the Oedipal situation poses another question. Will our love survive knowledge, particularly our growing awareness of the separateness of our love objects and their relationships with others which exclude us? When we seriously doubt that our capacity to love will survive this knowledge we are tempted to take refuge in the cultivation of illusions. Favoured among these are the many varieties of Oedipal illusion in which the phantasy of remaining the chosen one is perpetuated and kept secret. In some people, life, instead of being lived, can become the vehicle for the reinstatement of such defensive illusions, and the relationships of the external world are used only as stage props for an insistent internal drama whose function is to deny the psychic reality of the depressive position and the pains of the real Oedipus situation. It was with such patients that psychoanalysis began, in the *Studies on Hysteria.*

4

The equilibrium between the paranoid-schizoid and the depressive positions

JOHN STEINER

Certain portions of this chapter have already been published in a paper entitled 'The defensive function of pathological organizations', in B.L. Boyer and P. Giovacchini (eds), *Master Clinicians on Treating the Regressed Patient*, New York: Jason Aronson (1990), 97–116.

Melanie Klein's differentiation of two basic groupings of anxieties and defences, the paranoid-schizoid and depressive positions, is one of her important contributions to psychoanalysis. In this chapter I will try to describe what she meant by these terms and in the process illustrate how useful they can be when we try to orientate ourselves towards our patients in a clinical setting. I will then suggest that more recent work enables us to refine these concepts and to subdivide each of the positions to produce a more detailed developmental continuum which retains the dynamic notion of an equilibrium.

The two basic positions

Perhaps the most significant difference between the two positions is along the dimension of increasing integration which leads to a sense of wholeness both in the self and in object relations as the depressive position is approached. Alongside this comes a shift from a preoccupation with the survival of the self to a recognition of dependence on the object and a consequent concern with the state of the object.

In fact, each of the positions can be compared along almost any dimension of mental life and in particular in terms of characteristic anxieties, defences, mental structures, and types of object relation. Moreover, a variety of other features such as the type of thinking, feeling, or phantasying characterize the positions and each can be considered to denote 'an attitude of mind, a constellation of conjoint phantasies and relationships to objects with characteristic anxieties and defences' (Joseph 1983).

The paranoid-schizoid position

In the paranoid-schizoid position anxieties of a primitive nature threaten the immature ego and lead to the mobilization of primitive defences (Klein 1946). Klein believed that the individual is threatened by sources of destructiveness from within, based on the death instinct, and that these are projected into the object to create the prototype of a hostile object relationship. The infant hates, and fears the hatred of, the bad object, and a persecutory situation develops as a result. In a parallel way primitive sources of love, based on the life instinct, are projected to create the prototype of a loving object relationship.

In the paranoid-schizoid position these two types of object relationship are kept as separate as possible, and this is achieved by a split in the object which is viewed as excessively good or extremely bad. States of persecution and idealization tend to alternate, and if one is present the other is usually not far away, having been split off and projected. Together with the split in the object the ego is similarly split and a bad self is kept as separate as possible from a good self.

In the paranoid-schizoid position the chief defences are splitting, projective identification, and idealization; the structure of the ego reflects the split into good and bad selves in relationship with good and bad objects, and object relationships are likewise split. The ego is poorly integrated over time so that there is no memory of a good object when it is absent. Indeed the loss of the good object is experienced as the replacement of an idealized situation by a persecutory one. Similarly in the spatial dimension self and objects are viewed as being made up of parts of the body such as the breast, face, or hands and are not yet integrated into a whole person.

Paranoid-schizoid defences also have a powerful effect on thinking and symbol formation. Projective identification leads to a confusion between self and object and this results in a confusion between the symbol and the thing symbolized (Segal 1957). The concrete thinking which arises when symbolization is interfered with leads to an increase in anxiety and in rigidity.

The depressive position

The depressive position represents an important developmental advance in which whole objects begin to be recognized and ambivalent impulses become directed towards the primary object. The infant comes to recognize that the breast which frustrates him is the same as the one which gratifies him and the result of such integration over time is that ambivalence – that is, both hatred and love for the same object – is felt. These changes result from an increased capacity to integrate experiences and lead to a shift in primary concern from the survival of the self to a concern for the object upon which the individual depends. This results in feelings of loss and guilt which enable the sequence of experiences we know as mourning to take place. The consequences include a development of symbolic function and the emergence of reparative capacities which become possible when thinking no longer has to remain concrete.

The equilibrium PS ⟷ D

Although the paranoid-schizoid position antedates the depressive position and is more primitive developmentally, Klein preferred the term 'position' to Freud's idea of stages of development because it emphasized the dynamic relationship between the two. A continuous movement between the two positions takes place so that neither dominates with any degree of completeness or permanence. Indeed it is these fluctuations which we try to follow clinically as we observe periods of integration leading to depressive position functioning or disintegration and fragmentation resulting in a paranoid-schizoid state. Such fluctuations can take place over months and years as an analysis develops but can also be seen in the fine grain of a session, as moment-to-moment changes. If the patient makes meaningful progress, a gradual shift towards depressive position functioning is observed, while if he deteriorates we see a reversion to paranoid-schizoid functioning such as occurs in negative therapeutic reactions. These observations led Bion (1963) to suggest that the two positions were in an equilibrium with each other rather like a chemical equilibrium, and he introduced the chemical style of notation PS ⟷ D. This way of putting it emphasizes the dynamic quality and focuses attention on the factors which lead to a shift in one direction or another.

PATIENT A

To clarify some of these notions I will present some clinical fragments, first from a consultation interview with a patient operating chiefly at a paranoid–schizoid level.

From the beginning of the session the patient was consumed with anger. His wife had had several breakdowns requiring hospital admission, and a social worker had been seeing them as a couple. She had then arranged for his wife to have individual treatment and the patient was furious and arranged his own referral to the Tavistock Clinic. He was able to say very little about himself and when I pointed this out he became indignant, saying that he thought it unreasonable for a patient who had problems in communication to be expected to communicate. After several attempts to get through to him which led nowhere I asked for a dream. He described one in which he met a friend and was offered a lift home on his motorbike. They drove all over London and ended up at the river which was nowhere near his home. In the dream he got angry and said it would have been quicker to go home by himself. I interpreted that this was the feeling in the session where I was taking him all over the place but not where he wanted to go. I suggested that he was fed up and wondered why he had come at all. To this he said, 'Very clever'.

When I asked for an early memory he described several vaguely, but when pressed for detail he recalled a time as a small child when someone gave him a glass to drink from. He bit completely through it and ended up with pieces of glass in his mouth. Before that he thought he had been used to flexible plastic cups. I linked this with his rage in the session and his fear that things around him were cracking up. I interpreted that he was afraid I couldn't be flexible like the plastic cup, but might crack up as his wife had done. He was able then to acknowledge his violence and to admit that he hit his wife and also smashed the furniture at home. It remained impossible to work with him since to be flexible seemed to mean to become completely pliable and allow him to dictate how the session and his treatment should be conducted.

I felt that his arrogant and demanding nature reflected his need to avoid his internal chaos and confusion. He did not know how to cope with his wife's illness, perhaps because it reminded him so vividly of his own. Any relinquishment of his angry omnipotence threatened to expose the chaos and confusion.

Differentiation within the paranoid–schizoid position

The contrast between the two positions has an impressive clarity and simplicity and has proved to be extremely useful. In practice, however, we find defences being deployed in more complex ways, and a deeper understanding of mental mechanisms has led to a distinction between different levels of organization within the paranoid–schizoid position. In particular we are able to recognize normal splitting as only one aspect of the paranoid–schizoid position and to distinguish this from pathological fragmentation which can occur as a more primitive state involving fragmentation of the personality (Bion 1957; Segal 1964).

Schematically it is possible to divide the paranoid–schizoid position into a position involving pathological fragmentation and one of normal splitting as follows:

Pathological fragmentation $\longleftrightarrow$ Normal splitting $\longleftrightarrow$ Depressive position

Normal splitting

Melanie Klein has stressed the importance of normal splitting for healthy development (Segal 1964). The immature infant has to organize his chaotic experience, and a primitive structure to the ego is provided by a split into good and bad. This reflects a measure of integration which allows a good relationship to a good object to develop by splitting off destructive impulses which are directed towards bad objects. This kind of splitting may be observed clinically, and in infant observation, as an alternation between idealized and persecutory states. If successful the ego is strengthened to the point where it can tolerate ambivalence, and the split can be lessened to usher in the depressive position. Although idealized, and hence a distortion of reality, the periods of integration, which at this stage take place in relation to good objects, can be seen as precursors of the depressive position.

Pathological fragmentation

Although normal splitting can effectively deal with much of the psychic threat facing the individual, it frequently fails to master all the anxiety, even in relatively healthy individuals, and defences are called on which are more extreme and damaging in their effects. One such situation arises if persecutory anxiety becomes excessive, which may leave the individual feeling that his very survival is threatened. Such a threat may paradoxically lead to further defensive fragmentation which involves minute splitting and violent projection of the fragments. Bion (1957) has described how this leads to the creation of bizarre objects which intensify the persecution of the patient through experiences of a mad kind.

The result is intense fear, and a sense of chaos and confusion which may be observed clinically in extreme states of panic with depersonalization and derealization, where the patient describes feelings of being in tiny pieces or of being assaulted by strange experiences, sometimes in the form of hallucinations. The individual may yet tolerate such periods of extreme anxiety if the split can be maintained so that good experiences can survive. If splitting breaks down, however, the whole personality may be invaded by anxiety which can result in an intolerable state with catastrophic consequences. Such a breakdown of splitting is particularly threatened if envy is prominent, since destructive attacks are then mounted against good objects, and it is impossible to keep all the destruction split off. A confusional state may then develop which often has particularly unbearable qualities (Klein 1957; Rosenfeld 1950).

PATIENT B

A twenty-five-year-old artist would become irrationally terrified that his plumbing would leak, that his central heating would break down, that his telephone would be cut off, and so on. He was extremely anxious to start analysis and immediately became very excited, convinced that he was my star patient and wondered if I was writing a book about him. Very quickly, however, he felt trapped and insisted on keeping a distance by producing breaks in the analysis which created an atmosphere where I was invited to worry about him and prevent him from leaving. The extent of his claustro-agoraphobic anxieties was illustrated when he went to Italy for a holiday. Because of his country of origin he needed a visa, and although he knew this he had simply neglected to get one. When the immigration officials in Rome told him that he would have to return to London he created such a scene, crying and shouting, that they relented and let him in. Once in the country, however, he became frightened that he wouldn't be allowed out because the officials would see that his passport had not been stamped. He therefore managed to cajole his friends to take him to the

French border which he crossed in the boot of their car, obtained the necessary visa and re-entered in the normal way to continue his holiday.

It is clear that he regularly left me to carry the worry and concern for him, and this became particularly so when he behaved in a similar way when he took a holiday to the Soviet Union. This time he found that his visa did not correctly match the departure date and he simply took a pen and altered it. He did return safely and soon after had the following dream. He was in a Moscow hotel with a homosexual friend and wanted to masturbate with him. Two lady guides, however, refused to leave the room and indeed were proud of their work and of the hotel, even arranging to serve excellent meals in the room. The patient complained about this because he felt trapped, not even being allowed to go to the restaurant, and even began to suspect that the guides had connections with the KGB.

The panic which constantly afflicted this patient was basically that which resulted when things got out of control. His defensive organization was an attempt to deal with this chaotic anxiety by omnipotent methods in which he would force himself into his objects and then feel claustrophobic and have to escape in great anxiety. His dream of the Soviet Union did seem to contain a representation of a good object in the form of the two lady guides, perhaps representing the analysis, who served excellent meals, but his basic reaction to these was persecutory, and he complained that he was imprisoned and not allowed to go to the restaurant. What the guides did was interfere with his homosexual activity by their presence and I think this is what the analysis was beginning to do.

Differentiation within the depressive position

Splitting is not restricted to the paranoid–schizoid position (Klein 1935; 1952a; 1957) and is resorted to again when the good object has been internalized as a whole object and ambivalent impulses towards it lead to depressive states in which the object is felt to be damaged, dying, or dead and 'casts its shadow on the ego' (Freud 1917). Attempts to possess and preserve the good object are part of the depressive position and lead to a renewal of splitting, this time to prevent the loss of the good object and to protect it from attacks.

The aim in this phase of the depressive position is to deny the reality of the loss of the object, and this state of mind is similar to that of the bereaved person in the early stages of mourning. In mourning it appears as a normal stage which needs to be passed through before the subsequent experience of acknowledgement of the loss can take place.

An important mechanism deployed in this denial is a type of projective identification which leads to possession of the object by identifying with it (Klein 1952a: 68–9). Freud himself (1941) suggested that the notion of 'having an object' was later than the more primitive one of 'being the object' and relapses to 'being' after a loss. He wrote: 'Example: the breast. "The breast is part of me, I am the breast." Only later: "I have it" – that is, "I am not it"' (Freud 1941: 299).

A critical point in the depressive position arises when the task of relinquishing control over the object has to be faced. The earlier trend, which aims at possessing the object and denying reality, has to be reversed if the depressive position is to be worked through, and the object is to be allowed its independence. In unconscious phantasy this means that the individual has to face his inability to protect the object. His psychic reality includes the realization of the internal disaster created by his sadism and the awareness that his love and reparative wishes are insufficient to preserve his object which must be allowed to die with the consequent desolation, despair, and guilt. Klein put it as follows:

> Here we see one of the situations which I described above, as being fundamental for 'the loss of the loved object'; the situation, namely, when the ego becomes fully identified with its good internalized objects, and at the same time becomes aware of its own incapacity to protect and preserve them against the internalized persecuting objects and the id. This anxiety is psychologically justified.
>
> (Klein 1935: 265)

These processes involve intense conflict which we associate with the work of mourning and which result in anxiety and mental pain.

The depressive position can thus also be seen to contain gradations within it, particularly in relation to the question of whether loss is feared and denied or whether it is acknowledged and mourning is worked through. I have used this distinction to divide the depressive position into a phase of *denial of loss of the object* and a phase of *experience of the loss of the object* as follows:

Paranoid-schizoid position	$\longleftrightarrow$	Fear of loss of the object	$\longleftrightarrow$	Experience of loss of the object

Mourning

Freud (1917) has described the process of mourning in beautiful detail, and emphasizes that in the work of mourning it is the reality of the loss which has so painfully to be faced. In the process every memory connected with the bereaved is gone over and reality-testing applied to it until gradually the full force of the loss is appreciated. 'Reality-testing has shown that the loved object no longer exists, and it proceeds to demand that all libido shall be withdrawn from its attachments to that object' (Freud 1917: 244).

And later:

> Each single one of the memories and situations of expectancy which demonstrate the libido's attachment to the lost object is met by the verdict of reality that the object no longer exists; and the ego, confronted as it were with the question whether it shall share this fate, is persuaded by the sum of the narcissistic satisfactions it derives from being alive to sever its attachment to the object that has been abolished.
>
> (Freud 1917: 245)

If successful this process leads to an acknowledgement of the loss and a consequent enrichment of the mourner. When we describe the mourning sequence in more detail it can be seen to involve two stages which correspond to the two subdivisions of the depressive position I have outlined above.

First, in the early phases of mourning the patient attempts to deny the loss by trying to possess and preserve the object, and one of the ways he does this, as we have seen, is by identification with the object. Every interest is abandoned by the mourner except that connected with the lost person, and this total preoccupation is designed to deny the separation and to ensure that the fate of the subject and the object is inextricably linked. Because of the identification with the object the mourner believes that if the object dies then he must die with it and, conversely, if he is to survive then the reality of loss of the object has to be denied.

The situation often presents as a kind of paradox because the mourner has somehow to allow his object to go even though he is convinced that he himself will not survive the loss. The work of mourning involves facing this paradox and the despair associated with it. If it is successfully worked through, it leads to the achievement of separateness between the self and the object because it is through mourning that the projective identification is reversed and parts of the self previously ascribed to the object are returned to the ego (Steiner 1990). In this way the object is viewed more realistically, no longer distorted by projections of the self, and the ego is enriched by re-acquiring the parts of the self which had previously been disowned.

Klein (1940) has described this process vividly in the patient she calls Mrs A who lost her son and after his death began sorting out her letters, keeping his and throwing others away. Klein suggests that she was unconsciously trying to restore him and keep him safe, throwing out what she considered to be bad objects and bad feelings. At first she did not cry very much and tears did not bring the relief which they did later on. She felt numbed and closed up, and she also stopped dreaming as if she wanted to deny the reality of her actual loss and was afraid that her dreams would put her in touch with it.

Then she dreamed that she saw a mother and her son. The mother was wearing a black dress and she knew that her son had died or was going to die. This dream put her in touch with the reality not only of her feelings of loss but of a host of other feelings which the associations to the dream provoked, including those of rivalry with her son who seemed to stand also for a brother, lost in childhood, and other primitive feelings which had to be worked through.

Later she had a second dream in which she was flying with her son when he disappeared. She felt that this meant his death, that he was drowned. She felt as if she too were to be drowned – but then she made an effort and drew away from the danger back to life. The associations showed that she had decided that she would not die with her son, but would survive. In the dream she could feel that it was good to be alive and bad to be dead and this showed that she had accepted her loss. Sorrow and guilt were experienced but with less panic since she had lost the previous conviction of her own inevitable death. (This description is particularly poignant because Melanie Klein wrote this paper after she had lost her own son in a mountaineering accident, and it is clear that Mrs A of the paper was actually herself.)

We can see that the capacity to acknowledge the reality of the loss, which leads to the differentiation of self from object, is the critical issue which determines whether mourning can proceed to a normal conclusion. This involves the task of relinquishing control over the object and means that the earlier trend which was aimed at possession of the object and denying reality has to be reversed. In unconscious phantasy this means that the individual has to face his inability to protect the object. His psychic reality includes the realization of the internal disaster created by his sadism and the awareness that his love and his reparative wishes are insufficient to preserve his object which must be allowed to die, with the consequent desolation, despair, and guilt. These processes involve intense mental pain and conflict, which it is part of the function of mourning to resolve.

PATIENT C

I will briefly mention another patient who had a long and very stuck analysis dominated by the conviction that it was imperative for him to become a doctor. In fact he was unable to get a place at medical school, and after various attempts to study dentistry had to be content with a post as a hospital administrator, which he hated. Session after session was devoted to the theme of his wasted life and the increasingly remote possibility that studies at night school might lead to a place at a medical school, perhaps if not in Britain then overseas.

I was able repeatedly to link his need to be a doctor to his conviction that he contained a dying object in his inner world which he considered he had to cure and preserve and that he could not accept his inability to do so. He could not recognize that this task was impossible and quite beyond his power and he could not get on with his life and let his object die. He had a terrible fear that he would not be able to cope when his parents died and also a great fear of his own ageing and death. Somehow he was convinced that if he could be a doctor it would also mean that he would be immune from illness.

When he was fourteen his grandmother developed a terrible fatal illness in which she gradually and slowly became paralysed and died. My patient could not bear to see this go on and especially could not bear to watch the loving way his grandfather cared for his wife. When the doctor broke the news to the family he ran out of the house in a panic. I had heard different references to this tragic experience over the years, and one day I interpreted that his wish to be a doctor was an omnipotent wish to reverse this death and that he believed that he could even now keep his grandmother alive and was doing so inside him through the fantasy that as a doctor he would cure her. He was for a moment able to follow me and seemed touched, but a few minutes later explained that his wish to be a doctor had occurred not then but years earlier at the age of five after he had had his tonsils out. He described his panic as the anaesthetic mask was applied, and I have no doubt that he was afraid that he was going to die. The wish to be a doctor was therefore connected with the wish to preserve his own life as well as that of his objects, and the two were so inextricably linked that he could not consider that he could survive if his objects were to die. The task of mourning could not proceed and the idea of relinquishing the ambition of being a doctor was tantamount to giving up the wish to live.

This patient seemed stuck in the first phase of the depressive position, in which the fear of loss of the object dominated his defensive organization so that mourning could not be worked through. There were of course transient moves towards relinquishing his objects and also frequent regression to paranoid-schizoid levels of organization when paranoid fears dominated.

PATIENT D

In other patients, even early in our contact with them, evidence of the capacity to face the experience of loss becomes apparent. This seemed to be the case with a student who was referred for psychotherapy by a psychiatrist following an admission to hospital because of depression and suicidal ruminations. He gradually improved and returned to his home but was undecided if he should continue his studies. He came to the consultation obviously anxious and within a few seconds became extremely angry, perhaps because I had so far remained silent. When I asked him if he wanted to begin he grimaced and snapped, 'No!' At first I thought he looked quite psychotic since his lips were trembling with rage and he had great difficulty controlling himself. After a few minutes he got up and walked about the room looking at my books and pictures and eventually stopped and picked up a picture of two men playing cards and said, 'What game do you think these two are playing?' I interpreted that he felt he and I were playing a game and he wanted to know what was going on. He relaxed slightly and sat down again. He then said he felt I was adopting a technique which was imposed on me by the Tavistock Clinic and that I expected him to go along with it. I interpreted that he saw me as a kind of robot who mechanically did what I was told and he agreed.

When I asked for a dream he described one he had when he was fifteen and which remained extremely vivid. In the dream he was standing in a city which had been completely destroyed. Around him were rubble and twisted metal, but there were also small puddles of water and in these a rainbow was reflected in brilliant colours. I interpreted that he felt a kind of triumph if he could destroy me and make out of me a robot, which meant to him that I was simply twisted metal with nothing human about me. He admitted that the mood in the dream was ecstatic, and I suggested that the triumph and exaltation were a way of denying the despair and destruction. He relaxed perceptibly, and with additional work we could link the catastrophe in the dream to a time at the age of fifteen when he returned home to be told that his parents were going to separate.

In contrast to the earlier examples, I think the underlying situation in this patient was fundamentally a depressive one. His internal world contained damaged and destroyed objects which gave it the desolated appearance of a destroyed city. This filled him with such despair that he could not face it and was led to deploy manic mechanisms as a defence. If the mania and omnipotence could be contained he was able to make contact with his depression, which centred on his parents' separation, and work with the therapist.

Summary

The idea of a continuum between the paranoid-schizoid and the depressive positions is expanded to include subdivisions of each. An equilibrium diagram can be constructed as follows:

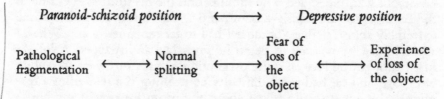

Each position can be thought of as in equilibrium with those on either side of it, and attempts can thus be made to follow movement between them in the course of a session and over the weeks, months, and years of an analysis.

5

Clinical experiences of projective identification

ELIZABETH BOTT SPILLIUS

I am grateful to several colleagues, particularly John Steiner, for helpful discussions of this chapter.

In this chapter I describe briefly the way Klein's introduction of the concept of projective identification has led to developments in technique. I focus mainly on work in England and mainly on that of Kleinian analysts, even though the concept has undoubtedly influenced the clinical approach of many other analysts and one cannot say that the concept 'belongs' to any particular school. I will concentrate on my own clinical experiences of projective identification and on the way these experiences have led me to abandon fixed expectations and rigid definitions in favour of trying to be prepared to experience whatever forms of projection, introjection, and counter-transference come to life in the session.

Klein introduced the concept of projective identification in 1946 in her paper 'Notes on some schizoid mechanisms', which was her first and major attempt to describe conceptually what she called the 'paranoid-schizoid position', a constellation of anxieties, defences, and object relations characteristic of early infancy and of the deepest and most primitive layers of the mind. I cannot begin to do justice to the complexity and subtlety of the experiences Klein describes in this most seminal of her papers. Projective identification was by no means the central theme of the paper. Klein describes it as one among several defences against primitive paranoid anxiety, and her discussion of it occupies only a few sentences. She says:

Together with these harmful excrements, expelled in hatred, split-off parts of the ego are also projected onto the mother, or, as I would rather call it, into the mother. These excrements and bad parts of the

59

self are not meant only to injure but also to control and take possession of the object. Insofar as the mother comes to contain the bad parts of the self, she is not felt to be a separate individual but is felt to be *the* bad self. Much of the hatred against parts of the self is now directed towards the mother. This leads to a particular form of identification which establishes the prototype of an aggressive object relation. I suggest for these processes the term 'projective identification'.

(Klein 1946: 8)

Even this definition is not entirely accurate, for Klein makes it clear in the course of her paper that the individual has phantasies of projecting good feelings as well as bad, so that the object is then felt to be good and the infant or patient then takes in a good object, which helps with the task of integration. But both in Klein's work and that of subsequent analysts the emphasis has been on the projection of bad feelings that the infant or patient cannot contain.

It was Klein's view that the most basic and primitive anxiety of the paranoid–schizoid position is a fear of annihilation from within the personality and that, in order to survive, the individual projects this fear into the external object as a defensive measure. In the view of the infant (or patient) this makes the external object bad, and the object is then likely to be attacked. But often the idea of the external object, somewhat distorted by projection, gets taken inside the personality and the infant (patient) then feels that he is being attacked by an internal persecutor. Klein assumes that in early infancy and in the most primitive layers of the adult mind, there are extreme fluctuations between good and bad, with an attempt to keep them separate. Splitting, projection, introjection, and denial are the main defences of the primitive mode of functioning characteristic of the paranoid–schizoid position.

It is clear that Klein thought that normal splitting and the projective identification associated with it were necessary parts of development, and that without them the basic differentiation between good and bad and between self and other would not get firmly established so that the groundwork for the later depressive position would be impaired. In the depressive position self and other come to be clearly distinguished, the individual recognizes that the loved person and the hated attacked person are one and the same, and he begins to accept responsibility for his attacks.

Klein often speaks of 'excessive' projective identification in which the self is depleted by constant efforts to get rid of parts of the self, although she does not give a very clear idea of what exactly it is that leads to excessive projective identification in some cases and not in others. It is clear too that she thought of projective identification as the patient's phantasy. She did not think that the patient literally put things into the analyst's mind or body. It was also her view that if the analyst was influenced by what the patient was doing to him it was evidence of something the analyst was not coping with and meant that he needed to have more analysis himself; she had similar views about counter-transference, and did not welcome the extension of the term to mean the analyst's emotional response to the patient, a usage that Paula Heimann introduced in 1950. Klein thought that such extension would open the door to claims by analysts that their own deficiencies were caused by their patients. It is still generally accepted, at least by British Kleinian analysts, that projective identification is a phantasy not a concrete act, but it is now accepted that patients can behave in ways that get the analyst to feel the feelings that the patient, for one reason or another, cannot contain within himself or cannot express in any other way except by getting the analyst to have the experience too (cf. Rosenfeld 1971; Segal 1973; Sandler 1976a, 1976b, 1987b; Sandler and Sandler 1978; Joseph 1985, 1987; Spillius (ed.) 1988: 81–6).

Klein's colleagues, especially Rosenfeld, Bion, Segal, Money-Kyrle, and Joseph, began using the idea of projective identification almost at once, though the actual term was not used very much until about the mid-1950s, and few papers were written specifically about the concept itself at this time. (For examples of use of the concept see Segal 1950, Rosenfeld 1952, Bion 1957 and especially 1959.) The concept gives an intellectual guideline for understanding and analysing the way the patient perceives the analyst, and gradually it has become part of the Kleinian focus on the analyst–patient relationship, particularly in understanding how the object relationships of the past, which in the present are part of the patient's internal world, are lived out in the analytic relationship.

In the 1950s in a brilliant series of papers Bion substantially added to the concept by making a distinction between normal and pathological projective identification (1957, 1958, 1959, 1962a, 1962b, 1970). He brought the object, the mother or the analyst, into the conception of the process of projective identification more than Klein had done. Following Klein, Bion thinks that when the infant feels assaulted by feelings he cannot manage, he has phantasies of evacuating them into his primary object, his mother. If she is capable of understanding and accepting the feelings without her own balance being too disturbed, she can 'contain' the feelings and behave in a way towards her infant that makes the difficult feelings more acceptable to him. He can then take them back into himself in a form that he can manage better. If the process goes wrong, however – and it can go wrong either because the infant projects overwhelmingly and continuously or because the mother cannot stand very much distress – the infant resorts to increasingly intense projective identification, and eventually may virtually empty out his mind so as not to have to know how unbearable his thoughts and feelings are. By this time he is on the road to madness.

Bion's distinction between normal and pathological projective identification and his formulation of the container/contained model have led to considerable development in technique. Although everyone agrees with Klein that the patient should not be blamed for the analyst's deficiencies of understanding, we are now much more prepared to believe that patients attempt to arouse in the analyst feelings that they cannot tolerate in themselves but which they unconsciously wish to express and which can be understood by the analyst as communication. Bion gives a brief example: he felt frightened in a session with a psychotic patient and then interpreted to his patient that the patient was pushing into Bion his fear that he would murder Bion; the atmosphere in the session became less tense but the patient clenched his fists, whereupon Bion said that the patient had taken the fear back into himself and now was (consciously) feeling afraid that he would make a murderous attack (Bion 1955). Similarly Money-Kyrle gives a description of a patient attacking him in a way that he could not easily understand and interpret, and it was not until after the session that he could disentangle his own contribution from his patient's so that in the next session he could make an appropriately 'containing' interpretation (Money-Kyrle 1956). Rosenfeld (1971; 1987), who has particularly studied projective identification in psychotic and borderline patients, stresses the importance of disen- tangling the many possible motives for it: communication, empathy, avoiding separation, evacuating unpleasant or dangerous feelings, taking possession of certain aspects of the mind of the other. (This last type has subsequently been called 'acquisitive' projective identification by Britton (1989) and 'extractive introjection' by Bollas (1987).) Riesenberg Malcolm (1970) describes the way she became aware of a patient's conscious perverse phantasy by feeling herself under pressure to be an audience for it, and indeed thus to be virtually a participant in it. O'Shaughnessy, especially in a paper called 'Words and working through' (1983), describes how projective identification can be an essential process of communication of experiences that a patient cannot capture in words.

Thus, unlike Klein, we are now explicitly prepared to use our own feelings as a source of information about what the patient is doing, though with an awareness that we may get it wrong, that the process of understanding our response to the patient imposes a constant need for psychic work by the analyst (see especially Brenman Pick 1985 and King 1978), and that confusing one's own feelings with the patient's is always a hazard.

Building on Bion's ideas, Joseph further stresses the way patients attempt to induce feelings and thoughts in the analyst, and try, often very subtly and without being aware of it, to 'nudge' the analyst into acting in a manner consistent with the patient's projection (Joseph 1989). Compare also Sandler's concept of 'actualization', a less colloquial term for the same process (1976a). Joseph gives many detailed examples. A masochistic patient, having in unconscious phantasy projected into his analyst a sadistic aspect of himself or of an internal object, will act in a manner that unconsciously tries to induce the analyst to make slightly sadistic interpretations. An apparently passive patient will try to get the analyst to be active. An envious patient will describe situations of which the analyst might well be expected to be envious. The analyst's aim is to allow himself or herself to experience and respond internally to such pressures from the patient enough to become conscious of the pressure and of its content so that he can interpret it, but without being pushed into gross acting out (Joseph 1989). Some degree of acting out by the analyst, however, is often inevitable in the early stages of becoming aware of what the patient is feeling, a point further stressed by O'Shaughnessy (1989).

I shall not attempt to describe the great proliferation of papers on projective identification that has developed since the 1960s, especially in the United States; Malin and Grotstein 1966; Jacobson 1967; Ogden 1979, 1982; Kernberg 1975, 1980, 1987; Meissner 1980, 1987; Grotstein 1981a; Sandler (ed.) 1987a gives a relevant collection of papers on the topic, and Hinshelwood (1989) gives a detailed discussion of Kleinian and later usages. Much of the American discussion has concerned the motive for projective identification (evacuation, gaining control, acquisition, avoiding separation) and with making a distinction between projection and projective identification, though I think that such a distinction is impossible to maintain or even to secure agreement on.

In Britain, as I have described, I think there are what one might call three clinical 'models' of projective identification: Klein's own usage, in which the focus is on the patient's use of projective identification to express wishes, perceptions, defences; Bion's container/contained formulation; and Joseph's usage, close to Bion's, in which the analyst expects that patients will constantly bring pressure to bear on the analyst, sometimes very subtly, sometimes with great force, to get the analyst to act out in a manner consistent with the patient's projection.

Historically the distinctions between these models are important, but clinically we now expect that all three may well be operative at the same time. Even when the analyst feels himself to be little affected by his patient's projection, for example, a more detailed look at the material may reveal expressions that he missed and pressures he was not fully open to; the analyst is always affected to some degree by his patient's projection, there is always some 'nudging' by the patient to push the analyst into action, and inevitably there is usually some acting out by the analyst, however slight. The issue that is most important to the patient and in the analyst–patient interaction may vary widely from one clinical occasion to another, and all the models of projective identification I have described may be important in getting to the heart of the matter.

I will try now to illustrate with material from three patients the three models I have described and to show how all three models can be useful in understanding the crucial points of interaction in a session.

MR A

In this session I was using the idea of projective identification rather as I think Klein might have done. I thought my patient's perception of me was distorted by his unconscious phantasy of projecting aspects of himself and his internal objects into me. This involved in particular his inability to enjoy anything for its own sake.

Mr A was the eldest of three children of a Catholic family in a Latin country. He had a long-standing sense of grievance because he felt his parents preferred the other children, and indeed it seemed likely to me that he had been somewhat deprived emotionally as a child. He sought analysis because of work difficulties and a sense of meaninglessness in his life. After much struggle in the analysis, he had completed his first independent research project – he is a biologist – and it had been well received by his colleagues. But then he began to feel worse and worse, saying his research was not really creative or original, he did not belong anywhere, he felt utterly inert, he was fed up with me and with analysis because he felt so dead. In one session he had a sudden fantasy, which he described as 'grandiose', of developing his so-called small research into a major undertaking with a grant from America etc., etc. I said he was telling me this plan in a way designed to lure me into making some sort of punitive interpretation about his omnipotence as if he wanted me to belittle and ignore both the validity of his research and the work we had done together to make it possible. He proceeded to talk about something else as if he had not heard what I had said – he was being as lofty towards me, in other words, as he was in his research plan. In the next session he reported the following dream.

He was on his way home to his own country for a holiday. On the way he saw an accident but no one was badly hurt. Once home, he heard from a casual acquaintance that his close friend Mario had got married. Mario had not invited the patient to the wedding, and he felt dreadfully left out.

He woke feeling life was not worth living. He was utterly incapable of taking pleasure in anything. Most of his associations centred around his opinion that Mario was probably incapable of marriage or any kind of deep relationship.

I said I thought Mario represented that part of himself that had been incapable of any sort of relationship with me, but that in recent months this Mario aspect of himself had come into contact with me more and more, which he described in the dream as a marriage. It was even producing 'children' in the form of his research. I suggested that the non-Mario part of himself felt terribly left out of the growing alliance between Mario and me and it had been trying to re-assert its control over both of us.

He thought about this and then said he could not see why he should feel so left out by his getting better. After a short silence he said that Mario's mother was an immaculate, attractive woman, very nice to Mario's friends, and in fact she had hinted to the patient that she wished Mario were more like the patient. He thought Mario's mother wanted Mario to be successful and to get married, but only to prove that she was a successful mother, not for Mario's sake. I said he seemed to be saying that my growing relationship with the Mario aspect of himself was not to be trusted because I only wanted Mario to grow up and develop so that I could congratulate myself on being a successful analyst.

In subsequent sessions he was gradually able, at least partially, to recognize himself in the qualities he attributed to me and to Mario's mother – especially his grudging attitude towards his own and my enjoyment of the analysis and of his success.

On the surface, as I have said, I was using the idea of projective identification in this session rather in the way Klein defines it. My patient was projecting into me his own incapacity to enjoy his success so that I, like Mario's mother, was perceived as wanting to help him for my own sake, not his. I found this easy to understand and did not sense much change in my usual analytic state of mind. But looking at the material more closely, one can see other levels in it, closer to the sort of thing Bion and Joseph describe.

You remember that in the first part of the dream he saw an accident but no one was badly hurt; he was going home for a holiday. In the session of the day before there had been an 'accident', a 'collision' type of interpretation when I had said he was trying to lure me into attacking him, a collision which he had totally ignored in the session just as, in the dream, he was going on holiday, that is, he was leaving me behind. In other words, I think he had experienced this inter-pretation as somewhat attacking and humiliating in spite of the care with which I had phrased it. And in fact I think I was feeling more attacked by his devaluation of me and of his analysis than I realized, and more attacking in return than I knew. I was coping with his contempt and depreciation by going 'correct' on him, freezing into analytic propriety. This meant that everything I said was more or less appropriate but lacked empathy because it lacked awareness of his unconscious attempt to project his humiliation into me and to nudge me into attacking him in retaliation. Behind my easy adoption of Klein's usage, in other words, lay a potential for looking at the material from the perspective of Bion's and Joseph's usages. It took some time for me to realize that his getting me to *feel* despised was just as important a projection, and perhaps even more useful for under-standing his experience, than knowing about his projection of his inability to enjoy his and my success.

MRS B

This session was dramatic and painful – no question of maintaining my usual analytic stance on this day. In phantasy the patient was projecting a painful internal situation into me and acting in such a way as to get me to experience it while she got rid of it.

Mrs B had to be perfect and was extremely scathing towards herself if she was not. She had managed these perfectionist aspirations by never really trying so that she could always maintain she would have succeeded if she had tried. Or she attributed her success or failure to 'fate', accident, and so on. She had considerable learning difficulties and in analysis had a tendency not to listen. She also had a very cruel streak which usually showed itself only in dreams and phantasies. She had had a very difficult experience of separation in early childhood; the session I shall describe occurred shortly before an unusually long holiday break, which she was going to make even longer by going away for an additional few days herself, for the most 'realistic' of reasons. Some form of acting out at breaks was not unusual for her, and we had discussed and interpreted her response to it some weeks before the session I shall present. After these interpretations there followed two or three weeks of 'ordinary' sessions, and then gradually she became fed up and critical of herself, her analysis, and me, and I felt I did not fully understand why.

In the particular session I shall describe she came about ten minutes late and was silent for a long time. Eventually, on the basis of the quality of the silence, I said she gave the impression of feeling very negative and angry.

Again there was a long silence. At the end she launched into a description of a lot of inconveniences and minor grievances, mainly at work. She said it was a peculiar twist that analysis stirs things up in such a way that all these minor complaints turn into an attack here.

I said she wanted me to regard them as minor complaints, but ...

No, she said, only to know the difference between major and minor. (There was utter contempt in her voice.) There was a short silence, then she said, 'I don't know whether it's you or me, but in the past ten days it seems to me you just totally and utterly keep missing the point.' (Her tone was exceedingly scathing.) 'Yesterday you apparently didn't notice it was so painful for me to admit that I find analysis and everything you do so terribly uninteresting. I can't stand it.'

I waited a bit, then started to speak, but she broke in, 'Don't talk! [almost screaming] You're just going to repeat what I said, or you're going to alter it. You don't take things in, you don't listen to what I say, or you listen and you just want to hear it the way you want it to be and you distort it.' (There could hardly be a better description of what she did to my interpretations, but interpreting projection directly is not usually helpful, especially when a patient is in a flight of paranoia.)

(I was finding it hard to think, and I knew that my own self-doubt and feeling that I was a bad analyst were getting powerfully stirred up by her accusations. But I managed one small thought, which was that she must be feeling inadequate too, and that my leaving had a lot to do with it. Then came a second thought, that she hates herself for being cruel even though she gets excited by it. It felt to me as if I was like a damaged animal making her feel guilty, and she wanted to stamp me out.)

I said she couldn't bear for me to know how painfully attacking she is, how much she wants to hurt me, how cruel she feels; but she also can't stand it if I don't know, don't react. It means she is unimportant.

'Can't you realize,' she screamed, 'that I am totally and utterly uninterested in you! I don't care! I only care about myself. Take your pain to your analyst. Well, it's not my fault if you haven't got one.'

What I said, after quite a long pause, was that I thought she felt I treated her cruelly, with complete scorn and indifference, as if she was boring and utterly uninteresting, and that was why I was leaving her.

She felt that the only way she could really get this through to me was by making me suffer in the same way.

There was another long silence. Then she said, 'None of this alters my being tired and having too many things to do.' (She sounded like a slightly mollified but still petulant child.) 'I suppose', she went on, 'I am in a childish rage with you. I never could attack my parents, so I have to make up for it now.'

I thought this reference to the past, although probably true, was a way of evading what was happening now. I said I thought nothing felt right to her. If she felt she hurt me, it made her feel so cruel that she couldn't bear herself, and she got furious with me for being the cause of her attack. But if I wasn't hurt she felt ignored, as if she had no power or importance at all.

She then repeated the last part of this interpretation almost as if she had not heard me and that it was her own idea; that is, she said if she didn't hurt me it meant she was a nothing. She then talked very indignantly about being left on her own. I said she thought I was cruel for leaving her on her own so arbitrarily and that she therefore had a right to attack me in kind. But she also felt I was leaving her because she was so attacking. She muttered that at least someone ought to notice that leaving was happening, as if implying that I was ignoring it. I said I thought she felt I was ignoring the time of the session as well as the holiday, and in fact it was time to stop now.

I would hardly present this as an ideal session, but I think it is an example of the way a patient may have an unconscious phantasy of projecting an experience into the analyst and may act in a way that makes the analyst feel it. I felt utterly trodden on, mistreated, immobilized. This is I think how she felt (unconsciously) about my leaving her, and how she had felt at the time of her traumatic abandonment by her parents in her childhood.

What particular thing was it, I asked myself later, that had made her so unable to express herself symbolically in this session, so intent on *doing* it instead of thinking it? I think it was a combination of my holiday and my self-doubt that led to her acting out in the transference. These were the 'minor' and 'major' complaints whose difference she angrily thought I should have known. The holiday had started the process off. ('Someone ought to notice that leaving is happening.') In a sense my holiday was her 'minor' complaint, though with her background no holiday could really be considered minor. My holiday meant that she was going to be left, as she said of me, with no analyst to take her pain to; it was my fault. She replied in kind by extending the holiday herself. As I described briefly at the beginning, I made several interpretations about this process, which had happened in various forms on many previous occasions. Then the holiday topic was dropped for some time, after which she had gradually become more critical and attacking on a variety of topics not seemingly connected with the holiday break, and I began to be puzzled and then to be assailed by misgivings about the way I was working. She sensed my self-doubt, and I think felt unconsciously that she had injured me so badly that I was not standing up for myself properly and had become persecutingly beyond repair. This was her major complaint. My self-doubt was, I believe, very similar to her feelings of unlovableness when her parents had left her. It was also very similar to the picture she painted of her parents, who had cruelly left her but felt very guilty and self-critical about it. Failure, damage, and imperfection were rampant in both of us. Her answer was to get the worst of it into me and then attack and abandon me. She became the cruel me who was leaving her and the cruel parents who had left her, and I became the stupid, miserable child fit only for abandonment.

In this session I made some use, though imperfectly, of Bion's and Joseph's approaches to projective identification. What hindered me from linking my own self-doubt with by patient's feelings of worthlessness was the factor so nicely described by Money-Kyrle many years ago (1956).

> How exactly a patient does succeed in imposing a phantasy and its corresponding affect upon his analyst in order to deny it in himself is a most interesting problem. ... A peculiarity of communications of this kind is that, at first sight, they do not seem as if they had been made by the patient at all. The analyst experiences the affect as being his own response to something. The effort involved is in differentiating the patient's contribution from his own.
>
> (Money-Kyrle 1956: 342)

Bion makes the same point, perhaps a little less explicitly.

> Now the experience of counter-transference appears to me to have quite a distinct quality which should enable the analyst to differentiate the occasion when he is the object of a projective identification from the occasion when he is not. The analyst feels he is being manipulated so as to be playing a part, no matter how difficult to recognize, in somebody's (*sic*) else's phantasy – or he would do if it were not for what in recollection I can only call a temporary loss of insight, a sense of experiencing strong feelings and at the same time a belief that their existence is quite adequately justified by the objective situation without recourse to recondite explanation of their causation.
>
> (Bion 1952: 446)

And Sandler describes the process too:

> I want to suggest that very often the irrational response of the analyst, which his professional conscience leads him to see entirely as a blind spot of his own, may sometimes be usefully regarded as a compromise-formation between his own tendencies and *his reflexive acceptance of the role which the patient is forcing on him.*

(1976b: 46)

MR C

In this session I was looking out for the way the patient was subtly inducing me to feel and act in accordance with his expectations. In the middle of the session this worked reasonably well and he shifted from being preoccupied and uninterested to being emotionally involved. But by the end I forgot about interpreting his attempts to get me to act out and actually *did* some acting out instead.

This patient was the child of wealthy but very preoccupied parents who saw to it that he was physically cared for (there was a succession of servants) but seem to have had very little awareness that he might have emotional needs. The patient imagines that he lived in a little secluded world of his own, sitting in his corner playing with his toys, quite happy and self-sufficient. Later he spent a lot of time outside playing with the village boys until he was sent away to boarding school. I got no impression of his consciously protesting against parental neglect. He stressed, on the contrary, the cultural duty of respecting and honouring parents, which he had always done. He was almost always very polite to me, and, although he missed many sessions because of his work, when he did come he was punctilious about coming on time. He thought it very odd that I might expect him to be in any way disturbed by holidays or weekends, or even to notice them. Only ends of sessions sometimes bothered him; why should he have to stop just when he had got interested in something? He was often silent and preoccupied in sessions.

He arrived on a Friday saying he had been sitting outside in his car making phone calls on his car phone and couldn't leave his thoughts about them and concentrate on the session. He went on to say that really most of the sessions here are useless, nothing happens, but then sometimes something really does happen and is very important to him, but it's always when he feels that he is really here. It is like a dream world almost, then, the thing I've called his world of freedom.

Silence. I said, 'Where is that dream world now?'

He answered literally. He never remembers dreams well. He always knows he has them but can't remember them. This time he was having one and his little daughter woke him – it was a dream about his dogs. They were puppies. He bent down to pat one and it nipped him, in fact tried to bite him quite hard. He patted the puppy on the head again and said to someone, 'Would you believe it, that little puppy really daring to bite me like that!' There was a lot more but he can't remember.

He went back to talking about how he couldn't stop thinking about his phone calls and his busy weekend. He told me what he was going to do during the weekend. I found my mind starting to wander to my weekend. (This was my clue to what was happening – I was feeling an impulse to fit in with a nudge from my patient. He was the busy preoccupied father, I was the child who was managing his lack of interest in me by thinking about my weekend, my toys in my corner. I was the puppy.)

I said that he was leaving me and felt he couldn't be here, he was too busy with his own concerns. I said I thought he expected me to get involved in my own thoughts quite happily and just leave him to get on with whatever he was thinking and planning.

He was silent for quite a long time. Then he said that what I had said reminded him of a friend of his who is an inventor. This inventor says that he was very much left on his own in childhood, and he was so desperately lonely that he took to inventing things so as to drive away his loneliness. But he (my patient) was never lonely. He liked being alone. He didn't feel badly that his parents were so busy and didn't notice him.

I said: Similarly he doesn't feel badly when I leave him, as I was doing today, as it was Friday. On the contrary, he felt that it was he who was leaving me, and he expected me not to feel badly over his being so busy and not noticing me. He expected me to be happy in my little world and not to mind that he didn't notice me.

Silence. (I felt that now he was here and thinking about what was happening.) I waited for quite a long time, then said that I thought he felt he took advantage of his parents' neglect, that he felt he liked being in his little private world just as he expected me to like being in mine. But somehow he was also encouraging me to protest, to be a brave little puppy and give him a bite. He had given me a little pat on the head and thought it would be brave of me to protest.

Silence. You mean it might have been braver if I had?

I said I thought he did believe that, though he didn't often let himself be aware of it.

71

He sighed. It was nearly the end of the session. I felt I was losing his attention. And then he gave me a bite.

'Oh,' he said, 'I didn't tell you. I won't be here on Monday, I'm going hang gliding. That Italian professor wants me to leave it, I don't want to help him. It's the competition, I don't want to miss it. I suppose I should. He's so crazy he needs me to help.'

I said I thought he felt I was so crazy that I needed him to come to his session on Monday to look after me.

He laughed. 'But you *know* it's the time of year for my hang gliding,' he said.

I said it was time to stop now.

In this session, as I hope is clear from the material, I was watching out not only for how he perceived me, but also for the way he was trying to induce me to act in accordance with his expectations, as indeed I started to do when I found my mind wandering to my own weekend, but I was able to make interpretative use of that 'nudge' and my incipient response to it. But at the end I found myself acting out his expectation instead of interpreting it. When he made his little dog bite – 'Oh, I didn't tell you, I won't be here on Monday, I'm going hang gliding' – I snapped back at him, gave him a little bite of my own – 'You feel I'm so crazy that I need you to come back on Monday to look after me'. He was amused, as he had been in the dream when the puppy snapped at him, and I lost the chance to interpret that before my remark, just for a moment he was allowing *himself* to be the puppy and letting me be the parent whom he was biting. But perhaps what was more important was that my jokeyness interfered with the seriousness of the interchange. Whether he was biting me or I was biting him did not matter so much as the fact that for a little bit of time in the session we had been in emotional contact instead of each of us living in separate worlds, and my irony minimized the fact that this contact between us was being lost, a point I was able to come back to, however, in subsequent sessions.

In conclusion

I have described sessions with three patients illustrating slightly different ways of using the idea of projective identification clinically: Klein's way, which focuses on the effect of projective identification on the way the patient perceives the analyst; Bion's way, which includes Klein's usage but focuses also on the way the patient's actions induce the analyst to feel what the patient unconsciously wants him to feel; and Joseph's extension of Bion's usage to examine continuously the way the patient constantly but unconsciously 'nudges' the analyst to act out in accordance with the patient's internal situation. Joseph and Bion have extended Klein's model by emphasizing the interaction between patient and analyst. I think, however, that trying to make sharp distinctions between the use of one model rather than another is not likely to be any more productive clinically than the effort to distinguish projection from projective identification. Without being very much aware of it, the analyst is likely to use all three models for trying to understand the reality of a session and, similarly, further examination of sessions may reveal that use of one of the other models might have revealed more.

6

Splitting and projective identification

MICHAEL FELDMAN

The way in which the concepts of splitting and projective identification have evolved in Melanie Klein's work illustrates very well, I
think, the creative interaction between theory and clinical observation,
which runs through psychoanalysis. The concepts were developed to
help understand some of the clinical phenomena with which she was
confronted, and, once incorporated into a more general theoretical
framework by Klein and her co-workers, these ideas have significantly
expanded the range of clinical material with which we are able to
work.

I propose to give a fairly brief outline of the concept of splitting and
projective identification, and then to describe three clinical fragments
in which I think it is possible to see some of the ways in which they
operate, and their consequences for the patient and for the analytic
situation.

Klein saw splitting as one of the earliest defensive operations called
into play by the immature ego in an attempt to cope with intense
anxieties to which it was at times subjected. She believed that, from
very early on, the infant was capable of some form of phantasy, and that
one of the characteristics of these phantasies was that they were related
to objects. Thus the infant's early experiences of pleasure were
essentially linked to a notion of an object that was the source of
pleasure, and conversely the experience of distress was linked to a
notion of an object causing the distress.

The primary function of splitting is to segregate the objects
associated with good experience from those associated with bad, in
order to protect and preserve the good objects on which the survival
of the self depended. This involved both segregating off everything
perceived as harmful and dangerous internally, and/or projecting it
into the outside world.

Klein recognized, however, that the splitting process was not only something brought to bear on the way objects were perceived and organized, but, since the internal and external objects which inhabit the infant's world are essentially related to aspects of the ego, it follows that splitting also involves the ego itself.

As Klein put it:

I believe that the ego is incapable of splitting the object – internal or external – without a corresponding splitting taking place within the ego. Therefore the phantasies and feelings about the state of the internal object vitally influence the structure of the ego.

(Klein 1946: 6)

She goes on to say:

It is in phantasy that the infant splits the object and the self, but the effect of this phantasy is a very real one, because it leads to feelings and relations (and later on, thought processes) being in fact cut off from one another.

(Klein 1946: 6)

Klein saw projection as a way the ego had of dealing with anxiety by ridding itself of danger and badness – the psychic equivalent of expelling dangerous substances from the body. But, as we know from the way an infant or young child uses their excretory functions, these may not only be a way of freeing themselves from uncomfortable contents, but also form an important mode of interacting with someone else. These functions can be used aggressively to control, or to engage the other in a positive fashion. Thus, to recapitulate, if we believe that our perception and experience of objects implies a phantasy of the relationship between the object and a part of the ego, then the splitting of objects (at its simplest into good and bad) is inevitably associated with a corresponding split in the ego. Furthermore, the mechanism of projection, by which the organism strives to rid itself of harmful contents, will also involve the evacuation of part of the ego itself.

Klein came to use the term 'projective identification' to describe this process whereby the infant projects (primarily) harmful contents into his object (for example, into his mother), and by the same token projects those parts of his mental apparatus with which they are linked. In so far as the mother then comes to contain the bad parts of the self, she is not only felt to be bad, as a separate individual, but is *identified* with the bad, unwanted parts of the self.

The object may now be felt as threatening and potentially intrusive (containing as it does the infant's aggressive, intrusive qualities, and its

75

propensity to deal with things by projecting them into others). The infant may feel, caught up in this vicious cycle, the need to attack the mother further, or to withdraw in order to protect himself. The experience of the object containing parts of the self may also give rise to unpleasant, even panicky feelings of being trapped inside, and the claustrophobic anxieties we see in some of our patients can often be understood in this light.

Although it is not possible to go into all the ramifications of this process, I would like to mention that the projective identification may also involve good parts of the self – projected in love, or in an attempt to protect something valuable from internal attack. Up to a point, this process is a normal one, necessary for the satisfactory growth of our relationships, and is the basis, for example, for what we term 'empathy'. If it is excessive, on the other hand, there is an impoverishment of the ego, and an excessive dependence on the other person who contains all the good parts of the self.

This has been an interesting and important area of research and development in psychoanalysis over the past forty years, and many of the ideas which have evolved have been complex and difficult. In addition to the papers of Klein herself, there have been valuable contributions from Segal (1964), Bion (1959), Rosenfeld (1971), and Joseph (1987).

Rather than try to give a more detailed theoretical exposition, I should like to describe, fairly briefly, three clinical situations in which I believe it was possible to follow the operation of some of the mechanisms I have been referring to.

A patient, Mr A, arrived for the first session after a holiday and I noticed that he was moving and speaking in an unusually clear and business-like fashion. He said that when he had arrived in the waiting room, he had found another man there already (he knows that I share the premises with colleagues, and had occasionally seen other patients in the waiting room). He had not seen this particular person before, and it had disconcerted him at first. He thought I might have made a mistake, and double-booked two patients. He imagined me suddenly discovering my mistake, feeling terribly embarrassed, and not knowing how to cope with the situation. He speculated that I would probably ask one of my colleagues to go to the waiting room to call one of them out, and explain the situation to him, and then I would see whoever remained.

He portrayed me, in his mind, as confused, embarrassed, and, moreover, unable to face the muddle I had created, sending someone else to deal with it on my behalf. The patient found himself very rapidly in a position where he was calmly observing, without a momentary thought that perhaps *he* might have made a mistake.

Later in the session, it emerged that in the course of the previous week, during my absence, he had found himself getting into a terrible mess; he had lost his watch, he hadn't known what was going on, and he described a variety of other difficulties.

What dynamic mechanisms can be invoked to account for the situation which obtained at the start of the session? It seemed to me that the patient's knowledge and experience of his own state of confusion, his embarrassment about finding himself in a mess during the holiday, and his difficulties over time (expressed in his loss of the watch) became projected, in his phantasy, into me. After a momentary sense of discomfort within himself on encountering an unfamiliar person in the waiting room, he cured himself of the unwelcome and disturbing thoughts and experience, and behaved in an efficient and well-organized way, while (in his phantasy) his analyst had to summon help to rescue himself from a muddle.

As the session proceeded, and the patient found himself once more in a familiar and reassuring setting, I think he felt less driven to project these unwelcome mental states into me, and he began to be able to use his perceptions of me – my voice and manner – to recognize that I was probably *not* in a confused state of mind. This was accompanied by his recovering the knowledge and memory of his own distress and discomfort during the holiday, and also his apprehension about returning.

It was evident that what was projected, in his phantasy, into me, and taken as real properties of my mind at that time, was not the whole of the patient's mental contents. He preserved a way of functioning that was well organized, and could work out how I might set about dealing with the consequences of my mistake or confusion, in quite a complex and logical fashion, and he even seemed sympathetic towards me. We are thus evidently dealing with a split which has taken place in his mind, with part of his mental contents temporarily unavailable to him, but colouring his perceptions and his phantasy concerning me.

I should add that there was something slightly unusual about this example of projective identification with this patient. In the situation I have described, I actually felt confident that I *was* seeing the correct patient, at the correct time, and knew that the other person in the waiting room was a patient of my colleague. What my patient said did not, on this occasion, succeed in discomforting me, although on other occasions he could be more accurate about my state of mind, or choose more effectively what he might say or do to *affect* my state of mind, inducing me into impatience, uncertainty, anxiety, hope, or some other mental frame. In other words in many cases we are not merely dealing with the projection, in phantasy, into an object, so that the object acquires certain properties derived from the patient's mental state (which may 'fit' the object to a greater or lesser extent), but we are often dealing with an active and dynamic process whereby the mental state of the object is *affected* by the projection.

This formulation regarding what had happened at the beginning of the session seemed to be confirmed by material later in the same session. One of the events which had taken place during the holiday was that Mr A had moved to a larger office, on a different floor, within the organization where he works. He had actually moved out while the two people with whom he shared the office were away on leave. When they returned, they complained bitterly that he had left the place in a terrible mess – not just the area he had vacated, but the whole office was untidy and dirty.

While reporting this, Mr A sounded slightly injured. He acknowledged that there had probably been a *bit* of untidiness, but he added in an emphatic way that he had *intended* to clean it all up, he just hadn't found the time. He then went on to describe in a more and more emphatic way how unreasonable and neurotic his colleagues were in making such a fuss, and how intolerant and petty they were.

It became evident as he talked that he was assuming a condescending, even contemptuous attitude towards his colleagues. He had not only actually left a mess in their office, during their absence, but he began to portray them as being in a mess psychologically as well, while he assumed a position of detached moral and psychological superiority, from the security of his more spacious, clean office, on a higher level.

You will perhaps recognize this process as being almost exactly similar to the one he had used to deal with his momentary discomfort and confusion at the beginning of the session, which was subsequently related to the disorder *he* had actually been in during the latter part of the holiday. The story about the office made the situation very concrete – he described the way in which he actually vacated a place, leaving a mess dispersed into the space which belonged to other people, while he became the detached, slightly superior observer, watching the others getting into a stew. When he described the interaction with his colleagues at work, it was also very clear that his response to their complaints inflamed them even more, and may well have driven them into speaking or behaving in unreasonable ways, which then of course confirmed his view of them.

Finally I should like to mention the fact that, with this patient in the situation I have described, the projective identification seemed to have been 'flexible' or 'fluid'. In the session, the patient *was* able to recover, and speak about his own anxieties and confusion, without feeling terribly threatened by them, or attacked by me, when I interpreted what I thought was taking place.

I should now like to discuss a second case, Mrs B. Mrs B was the younger of two sisters, brought up by her mother under difficult circumstances, father having left the family when she was very young. Her mother, who was a highly disturbed woman, seems to have focused her hatred and violence on the patient.

In spite of the considerable internal and external difficulties which she faced, Mrs B had managed to make a success in various areas of her life. She is married, and has two young daughters. She has not, however, managed to free herself from the constant sense of being threatened by the image of an extremely hostile and envious mother. What she finds the most disturbing is the recognition of aspects of herself which remind her of her mother, particularly in her treatment of her own daughters. When she becomes aware of this, she feels a tremendous pressure to disavow these characteristics, either consciously through her conduct, or unconsciously through the projection of such features onto a figure in the outside world.

Mrs B arrived for a session in the middle of the week, and said there was something she felt she should have mentioned. She felt uncomfortable about not having done so – she wasn't quite sure why, perhaps she was waiting for the matter to be resolved. She then told me that a relative, with whom Mrs B has a complicated and difficult relationship, had unexpectedly offered to pay for her older daughter to attend a private school.

Mrs B was evidently uncomfortable and tense talking about this, and seemed unable to say much more. She said she supposed that she was worried that people might think the family were well off, which they weren't, of course. It was evident that Mrs B was apprehensive about my reaction both to what she had told me, and to the fact that she had avoided mentioning it for several days.

There were many features of the situation she described which reminded me of issues relating to Mrs B's own childhood and schooling, and her relationship with her mother. I was particularly reminded of the way she had lived in constant dread of her mother's explosive, even violent rages, and tried to propitiate her by behaving in a compliant, submissive way. Any achievement on her part, anything which she valued and enjoyed, seemed particularly likely to arouse her mother's resentment and envy. She had always assumed that this was because of her mother's own very deprived, poor background.

With some of this in mind, it was possible in the session I have referred to, to explore her discomfort about her daughter's move to a private school in terms of the envy which would be aroused in others who were less privileged. More immediately, I thought the marked tension and avoidance which she showed in relation to myself could be understood in terms of a phantasy of me as a figure who would react to her news by turning on her in a hostile and violent way, possibly even wanting to get rid of her, as she had often felt her mother did.

The patient could, and frequently did, tell herself that such fears were unreasonable and 'silly', and she knew I would not react like that, but such attempts to reassure herself did not mitigate her anxiety, or the harshness and severity of the figure which had been projected into me, and which felt very real. When I was able to interpret this to her, she visibly relaxed, as if this figure receded from the foreground, and she felt herself to be with a more supportive person.

She arrived for her session the next day, and I noticed that her face was red, blotchy, and swollen. She was evidently in some distress, and began by saying she hadn't wanted to come at all; she hadn't felt like telling me about her accident, she wasn't sure how I would react. She had tried to tell herself that it would be all right, I wouldn't mind, and she really ought to come.

There had also been a disturbing dream the previous night, which she felt she ought to talk about. She then told me a little about the accident. She was preparing some hot food in the food mixer which blew up in her face. She rather played down what had clearly been a frightening and painful experience. She went on quickly to tell me about the dream. In it, she thought some of the events of the previous evening were repeated, though she wasn't sure; then there were two figures – one was supposed to be looking after the other, but there was a quarrel, and the one supposed to be doing the looking after just pushed the other away, and probably killed her.

I should like to summarize briefly what evolved in the course of this session. Mrs B told me that she had felt somewhat relieved after the previous session, but some unease about the private school remained. What had made things much worse was the fact that she had then learned that her daughter had an interview with the new headmistress the following day. Mrs B would have to accompany her, and she didn't know how long it would take. She might come late for her session, or might have to miss it altogether. There was probably no way she could let me know what was happening. Mrs B is always very conscientious about being on time, and will strive to get to her sessions in the most difficult circumstances. On the rare occasions she is delayed or prevented from coming, she is always careful to telephone and explain, and apologize, as if constantly having to propitiate a very touchy, potentially explosive figure.

She thus found herself in an extremely difficult situation. She was just about able to cope with the anxiety that I would react in a hostile and envious fashion to the news about the daughter's school fees, perhaps demanding a higher fee for myself. There was then the additional provocation of the session she might miss or come late for, and in her phantasy, that would be the last straw – I was very likely to explode, like the mother she was so familiar with.

This became real in a dramatic way with the incident of the food mixer which exploded in her face, frightening and hurting her, and adding to her anxiety and reluctance to come, because she indicated that she half expected that I would be further provoked and annoyed by the fact that she came bringing all this trouble, and was unlikely to be sympathetic. The dream also represented the situation in which the figure who is supposed to provide care suddenly turns into a quarrelsome and rejecting person. At one level, of course, Mrs B doesn't believe this of me. On the contrary, in addition to the recognition of the fact that she has actually been helped a great deal, there also exists a rather idealized version of myself, as someone who can understand things perfectly, without her having to say very much, someone who is infinitely patient and helpful. This is an expression of splitting, where each version of the analyst can exist in an isolated way, without modifying the other to any great extent.

In the session I have been describing, I interpreted some of the patient's very real and concrete phantasies about me, and the way I might react, linked with the knowledge we shared both about her actual experience of her mother, and about the internal phantasy figure with which she lived. This seemed to restore her sense of having an analyst who *was* protective, and she left looking greatly relieved.

This illustrates, I believe, an aspect of what James Strachey put forward in his seminal paper of 1934 concerning the therapeutic action of psychoanalysis. The patient is able, in the transference, to project onto the figure of the analyst some archaic form (in this case that of an alarming, persecuting, and explosive figure), and in the course of the analytic work, through the analyst's understanding and interpretation, and his capacity to avoid getting caught up in a re-enactment of the phantasied situation, a modification of this primitive form, or imago, may take place, accompanied by a change in the patient's relation to it. The re-introjection of this modified figure gives the patient relief, and he feels less driven to resort to violent projective procedures, and this allows psychic change to occur.

The most difficult problem for my patient is, of course, that this archaic imago of the explosive, envious, and destructive mother has become incorporated into her own ego, through a process of introjective identification, but she finds it nearly intolerable to acknowledge this as part of herself and, as I have described, generally feels driven to enact the role of a tremendously patient, long-suffering, and 'good' figure – an example, perhaps, of Freud's description of the defence of reaction formation. The material I have given illustrates how, by means of projective identification, that part of her ego which is identified with her mother is projected into me, which makes me a fearful and worrying figure, which she is inclined either to avoid, or to try to appease.

It will be evident that the threat is much greater for Mrs B than for Mr A, and the need to disavow this aspect of her mental contents is consequently much greater. Thus, for example, when she spoke of the possible envious response of neighbours to her daughter's change of school, or her fears of how *I* might react, she seemed completely out of contact with any envious feelings *she* might have towards her daughter, and her own inclination (which sometimes manifested itself) to attack her daughter.

Returning now to the clinical situation which I have been describing, Mrs B did in fact miss the Friday session, as she had warned me she might. When she arrived on the following Monday, she explained the circumstances in a careful, polite, and terribly reasonable way. She explained how difficult it had been even to get to a telephone, leaving me in no doubt that she had done everything possible. I noticed she said nothing about the interview, or its outcome. As she went on speaking, I thought there was a rather superficial quality to it; she offered descriptions and explanations which sounded right and true, but somehow empty, and I felt I had heard it all before. There was no indication that she had any recollection of the work which had gone on in the last session, although it seemed relevant to her present predicament.

I found myself becoming frustrated and impatient with her as the session went on, and as she continued speaking in this sensible, considered way, with little emotion, and little sense of conviction. The patient herself commented at one point that it felt as if there was something missing. I began to feel that while, on the surface, we were both being reasonable and sensible, there was, at the same time, a subtle invitation to me to react in an impatient or critical way to what was going on, or what was being avoided.

However disturbing the image of her mother which we had previously encountered, there was a sense in which the patient felt very bound up with it, in a very alive way, and its absence made her feel there was *something* or *someone* missing. I had often noticed how in her everyday life some figure would assume the role of an angry, hateful, and unreasonable person, leaving Mrs B feeling hurt, puzzled, and victimized.

On this occasion I was able to recognize what I thought the pressure was, and felt I could see something of what was going on, rather than simply *react* to it, which was what took place on other occasions. I was able to interpret something of this to the patient, and she became much more uneasy, but more alive, and more *present* in the room. She then began to say how resentful she felt when I made these links, and addressed something which *I* thought was around but which she hadn't really been aware of. Suddenly she referred in a sharp, attacking way to an apparent inconsistency in my interpretation, which immediately revealed how much of our previous work was now available to her. She said, towards the end of the session, in which she had by then become very involved, that she felt quite *explosive*.

I think we can see here not only the projection into me of this violent and aggressive figure, but also a more subtle process whereby, unconsciously, she sought to re-create the familiar object relationship, in which she is the attacked and abused child of an angry, critical mother. This familiar, repetitive pattern, which is part of what Freud refers to under the heading of the repetition compulsion (Freud 1920), or Sandler describes as role actualization (Sandler 1976a; 1976b), serves to protect the patient from having to contain and take responsibility for her own envy, hatred, and violence, even if it leads to her feeling rather flat and empty. When, instead of enacting the role for which I was being cast, I was able to interpret it to her, she suddenly became more alive, though now she had to tolerate the anxiety and pain involved in owning these violent and destructive impulses and phantasies.

The third example is a brief one, which arose in the supervision of a young woman in psychotherapy with a therapist who is proving to be sensitive and gifted, with a real flair for the work he is engaged in. In the session prior to the one which was being reported, material had emerged which had enabled us to understand a stubborn provocative quality which the patient, a young woman, possessed, and which seemed to play a large part in the difficulties she experienced within her family and outside it. She arrived three or four minutes late for the next session, but made no reference to the fact that she had kept the therapist waiting. She began by saying she had been to a chemist's just before the session, trying out some perfume which she liked. She had *deliberately* kept the person behind her waiting a bit, while she tried out different brands.

The therapist was not quite sure what to do, and then alluded to the fact that perhaps she had kept *him* waiting in the same way, but the patient appeared not to know what he was talking about. There was some other material, and the therapist then made an interpretation, partly based on what had emerged in the previous session, about the way the patient sometimes behaved in a stubborn and provocative fashion. She said she hadn't properly heard him, although she thought he had said something very important, and would he please repeat what he had said. Rather than responding immediately to the pressure she put on him, the therapist waited a while, and the patient began to berate and challenge him, saying she supposed he *wouldn't* do what she had asked him, he would just sit there in silence, and make her wait, though she *thought* he had said something important.

It will perhaps be evident how the therapist was now being treated as a stubborn and provocative person, withholding something potentially helpful from the patient. I should like to examine this example in some detail.

Before the session, the patient seemed to have been quite aware of an impulse in herself to keep *someone* waiting deliberately, while she tried different kinds of perfume. She gave no indication of whether she was aware that, while doing this, she was also likely to keep her therapist waiting. When she did actually arrive late, and referred to the episode in the chemist's shop, it is difficult to believe she had *no* awareness of the link. It does seem, however, as if the responsibility for the knowledge both of her lateness and its possible motivation is made over to the therapist, who felt somewhat provoked, and driven to point out that she had kept *him* waiting. The patient apparently did not know what he was referring to.

Later in the session, he addressed directly her stubborn and provocative behaviour. It seems to me that something of his interpretation must have touched the patient, as she registered that he had said something important, but then instead of having to tolerate any discomfort, anxiety, or guilt about what he had identified as being located *in her*, she immediately projected into the therapist not only the qualities of stubbornness and provocativeness, but also the capacity to think, understand, and remember. She is thus apparently unaware that she was late, and seems to have lost touch with the recognition that she had deliberately kept someone waiting. She apparently puts pressure on him to behave in a *reasonable* and helpful way, by repeating his interpretation, although she has had enough experience of her therapist and his technique to know that he was unlikely simply to comply. If he had done so, I strongly suspect it would have had little or no effect.

On the other hand, by behaving in a way which she expects and indeed half invites him to, a familiar scenario is created in which the patient is the somewhat unfairly treated victim of a provocative and stubborn therapist. The therapist was able to recognize the pressures on him, and to refrain from simply acting out some role with the patient, but remained relatively well able to observe, think about, and comment on what was taking place. It became clear how she used projective identification to defend herself, but in addition, used a more complex defence in which the therapist is required to play a repetitive role in some internal drama of the patient – for example, to be the person who submits, a little resentfully, to the patient's demands, without believing it will do any good, or alternately, who resists this pressure and engages, instead, in angry recrimination and blame. To the extent that he allowed himself to be forced into acting in a certain way in response to such pressure, or as a reaction against the pressure, rather than maintaining an analytic posture, the therapist would support the patient's defence, where this internal situation is re-enacted over and over again. This would allow her to avoid having to think or to understand herself and her object relations better.

One further issue which this material raises relates not simply to her defensive use of splitting and projective identification, but, as I will mention a little later, to the communicative function of such mechanisms. The patient created, in the therapist, a very vivid experience of being made to wait for someone who was busy trying on perfume, who arrives in a somewhat haughty way, and does not know what he is talking about when he 'complains', as it were. There are some indications that what she is conveying to him, unconsciously, through this drama, is something of her own infantile experience, of having to wait while a rather provocative and narcissistic mother puts on perfume, while the child became impatient and frustrated. When she objects, her complaints are either not understood, not acknowledged, or not properly heard. When he made an effort to address her, there was something of the quality of a mother saying, 'What was that, dear? Tell me again', which leaves the child with no conviction that mother will really take in something, however many times it is repeated.

I should now like to bring together some of the aspects of splitting and projective identification which I believe the material from the three patients illustrates. First, to recapitulate: Mrs Klein used the term 'projective identification' to refer to what was essentially an unconscious, omnipotent phantasy, in which unwanted, disturbing mental contents were expelled – projected into an object – as a means of ridding the self of something bad, but also at times in order to attack or to control the object into which the projection occurred. Since a part of the ego is also expelled, the object which receives the projection also contains, and is partially identified with, a part of the self. The paradox is that although the object comes to be partially identified with a part of the self, the link between the self and that which has been projected

85

is disowned, so that the object is not recognized as having anything to do with the self, or what was projected, but is seen, as it were, to contain these qualities, motives, or functions *in its own right*.

The other aspect of this original definition of projective identification as an unconscious phantasy is that because it is an omnipotent phantasy, it takes place irrespective of the properties or responses of the object – the object does not need, as it were, to participate in the process. I think there are examples of this in all three patients I have described. Mr A found the discomfort, anxiety, and confusion of the holiday and his return to the analysis difficult to cope with and made it clear that he had, in phantasy, projected the muddle over time, the embarrassment, and the tendency to avoid the mess he had made, into me – before he had actually encountered me again. That part of himself which then dominated the scene was the part which functioned in an efficient and business-like way, not being bothered by anything. The contact with me during the initial part of the session, the diminution of his anxiety, and his capacity for reality-testing then altered the situation, and he recovered his contact with the confusion and mess which he had previously projected.

Mrs B forcefully projected an image of an intolerant, irritable, and envious person into me, and was thus reluctant even to face me with the news about her daughter's school, or subsequently to tell me about her accident, and the prospect of having to come late or miss a session. It became evident that the figure which was projected did not merely correspond to a very fixed imago of her mother, but included a part of the patient herself, identified with her mother, which she feared and hated. As long as this remained projected, there was a shallowness and stilted quality to the very polite, considerate, and sensible person who was talking to me. She feared and resented my interpretations which drew attention to the situation, and she felt quite disturbed at the prospect of having to *own* those aspects of herself, in relation to her own daughter, or her analyst, which she found so threatening and painful. She *could*, however, make use of interpretations which put her in touch with previously disowned parts of herself and she then came more alive, more three-dimensional, and could get relief from discovering that we could both survive, and the analysis could proceed.

Rosenfeld (1971) has made the important distinction between the use of projective identification as a means of evacuation, and as a means of communication. He made the point that if the former motive predominates, then any attempt at interpreting the material to the patient will not succeed, as the patient feels one is trying to push something unwanted back into him.

On the other hand, when projective identification is mainly being used as a means of primitive communication, the understanding of what is projected can be felt by the patient to be helpful – the patient may feel relieved that the analyst has been able to understand, and put him in touch with something which the patient could not, himself, either face or put into words.

I thought there was evidence for *both* with Mrs B, who first felt threatened and defensive, but as the session proceeded, it was evident that something important *had* been able to be communicated to me, and her paranoid anxiety diminished considerably.

Similarly, as I have suggested, in the case of the third patient, there was both the need to disavow her provocative stubbornness and its effects, which might have given rise to feelings of anxiety and guilt, but also to make the therapist have something of the experience of being a frustrated and tantalized child, confronted with a rather narcissistic, perfuming mother.

There is a further aspect of projective identification which we have come to understand better, as other analysts have built on Mrs Klein's original work. This concerns the way in which the projection is not only an internal phantasy, or used to communicate an emotional state or states of mind, but actually functions as a means of *affecting* the object, and influencing his behaviour. The subjective experience within the analyst is that he 'finds himself' saying or doing something under pressure. He feels forced or impelled, in a way which doesn't feel entirely comfortable or ego-syntonic. It is sometimes possible to recognize the pressure, or the induction of a puzzling state of mind, and to try to understand it, but at other times the pressure is either more subtle or more compelling, and the analyst finds himself responding to it.

In the case of Mr A, I was not aware that there was much pressure on me – I suspect that, partly because of the holiday break, Mr A was on this occasion unable to tune in sufficiently to what was going on between us to find an effective method of affecting me, and his need to convey something to me was too strong.

With Mrs B, as I have described, I found myself at one point becoming impatient and frustrated with her bland, slightly-too-good way of speaking and conducting herself, and it would have been very easy to make remarks which would have sounded critical. When I was able to recognize this, and use this recognition to make some sense of the situation, it seemed to be helpful. If I *had* behaved in a critical and impatient way, we would simply have re-created a familiar scenario in which she is the victim of an impatient and hostile figure.

It was very clear with the third case what pressure the therapist was under – to raise the issue of the patient's lateness which she was either unaware of, or had ignored, and then to respond to her request that he repeat his interpretation – either compliantly, or engaging with her in some process of mutual complaint.

We must, of course, be careful to avoid the temptation to 'blame' our patients for our own failure of understanding or technique, or the conflicts or sensitive areas which we ourselves possess, and it is all too easy to attribute most of the difficulties in an analysis to the patient's use of projective identification. It is always important to try to assess the contribution these other factors, which are to some extent the *analyst's* responsibility, make to the difficulties which arise.

However, the concept of projective identification which Klein formulated, and the development of the theoretical and clinical understanding of what is involved, by Bion, Rosenfeld, and others, has greatly increased the scope and power of the theoretical model, with important implications for clinical practice, as I hope I have been able to demonstrate.

7

Psychosis: not thinking in a bizarre world

EDNA O'SHAUGHNESSY

Bion often mentioned his indebtedness to Freud and Klein for the foundations of psychoanalytic thinking on psychosis. As an introduction to the exposition of Bion, I shall give the briefest of sketches of them both. Central to Freud's view of how psychosis differs from neurosis, and how neurosis in its turn differs from more normal states, is the ego's relation to reality. In its normal condition the ego is largely governed by what Freud called the 'reality principle', reality, internal and external, being made known to the ego by the senses, by consciousness and by thinking. In Freud's words:

> one of the features which differentiate a neurosis from a psychosis [is] the fact that in a neurosis the ego, in its dependence on reality, suppresses a piece of the id (of instinctual life), whereas in a psychosis, this same ego, in the service of the id, withdraws from a piece of reality.
>
> (Freud 1924b: 183)

That is, in neurosis the relation to reality is retained at the cost of instinctual repression, while in psychosis the relation to reality is lost. The psychotic ego has a need to find some substitute for the reality it has lost – for example, in a delusion – which Freud sees as an attempt at cure. Moreover, as a result of his researches, Freud also became convinced of a proclivity for psychosis in us all. He writes:

> From the very beginning, when life takes us under its strict discipline, a resistance stirs within us against the relentlessness and monotony of the laws of thought and against the demands of reality-testing. Reason becomes the enemy.
>
> (Freud 1933: 33)

The loss of reality, delusional attempts at cure, and intrinsic hatred of thought and reality are Freud's main ideas.

Klein approaches psychosis via anxiety. It is her view that our earliest anxieties are psychotic in content. The normal development of infants, she writes, 'can be regarded as a combination of processes by which anxieties of a psychotic nature are bound, worked through and modified' (Klein 1952a: 81).

However, in an abnormal infant the processes of binding, working through, and modifying do not take place, and the result is that primitive anxieties and terrifying figures remain unmodified and threaten to dominate the psyche of the infant and adult psychotic, so that the ego is driven to an excessive use of the otherwise normal defences of splitting and projective identification.

All these fundamental notions of Freud and Klein enter into Bion's theories: our hatred of reality and thinking, the ego's loss of reality in psychosis, its dominance by unmodified primitive anxieties, its use of the defences of splitting and projective identification, and its desperate search for cure. Bion put these discoveries and ideas in a different framework, a much more extreme version of the difference between psychosis and neurosis which had so struck Freud. According to Bion, in psychosis there is a difference in the entire condition of the mind and a difference also between the very constitution of what for the psychotic is the world.

Bion opens his paper 'The differentiation of the psychotic from the non-psychotic personalities' (1957) with this statement:

> The differentiation of the psychotic from the non-psychotic person-alities depends on a minute splitting of all that part of the personality that is concerned with awareness of internal and external reality, and the expulsion of these fragments so that they enter into or engulf their objects.
>
> (Bion 1957: 43)

According to Bion, the psychotic personality has its origin in the fragmentation followed by the expulsion of the *means* by which the ego knows reality; that is, the fragmentation and expulsion of the senses, consciousness, and thinking. This is the hinge of the difference. What could bring about such an eradication of the very aspect of the mind that is central to the institution of what Freud called 'the reality principle'? Bion thinks there are two preconditions for the psyche to institute psychotic functioning: first, a highly adverse inborn disposi-tion, and, second, its interaction with an adverse environment.

Such an adverse disposition will have the following features: a preponderance of destructive impulses, a never-decided conflict between the life and death instincts, anxiety at a horrific level so that, in Bion's words, 'there is a dread of imminent annihilation' (1957), plus a total intolerance of frustration. All these features are interrelated. At the outset of life frustration is concretely experienced as bad objects present. An infant with the endowment described will have bad objects of a terrifying order which raise anxiety to an horrific level for an embryonic personality which has anyway problems of toleration. The predicament of such an infant is very different from an infant with a better inborn disposition who faces and knows his frustrations and uses primitive precursors of thinking to modify them; for example, cries for his mother until she comes. The less fortunate infant, instead of facing his situation, evades it, in extreme cases completely. I have in mind an infant who lay in his pram in the garden from eight o'clock in the morning to late afternoon, not crying but gazing at the leaves of the trees. In his case a departure from functioning according to the reality principle has already set in. Instead of beginning to develop a mind for thinking, it is likely that such a psyche has become an apparatus for ridding itself of bad objects. It does this by the minute fragmentation and projection of incipient thoughts, sensations, and also the sense organs which threaten to bring awareness of internal or external reality. The infant in my example perhaps used his eyes as channels for projecting the unwanted fragments of his personality into external objects. On this model we can understand how the infant under the trees is free of hunger and terror because his psyche is in fragments in the leaves.

At this point a natural question arises: Why does his mother ignore him all day? Bion thinks that such an infant's situation is worsened by a mother who allows no ingress to projections. The infant experiences her refusal to take in his projections as hostile defensiveness, and will, Bion thinks, assail her with increasing hostility and frequency until in the end the meaning has been taken out of his projections. I believe a process of this sort was demonstrated to me by a psychotic adolescent boy who brought a boomerang to his session. He threw it, but it never returned to him and seemed to land nowhere in particular. He threw it ever more violently, with increasing despair, and I saw that the shape of the boomerang matched exactly the set of his mouth. The boomerang was a mouth, a cry which landed nowhere and brought him no return; thus he acted out his feeling that there was no object to understand and respond to his cry. Such an object, unavailable to receive projections thrown out by the infant, will be experienced as an additional external source of destruction of communication and awareness. My surmise is that such a mutually hostile and despairing situation had arisen between the infant who lay all day under the trees and his mother – a situation which the infant survived by instituting a psychotic state of mindlessness. It should be added that a constructive interchange even between a mother who accepts projections and an infant with a highly adverse endowment is intrinsically nearly impossible because all frustration is intolerable to her infant. Only her continuous presence will satisfy him, and in addition she will have to tolerate projections of an abnormal and violent kind.

However, were such an infant to have an object capable of receiving these projections and retaining what Bion called 'a balanced outlook', his situation would be to an extent ameliorated, although it will still be serious since the psychotic infant is then likely to be, in Bion's words, 'overwhelmed with hatred and envy of the mother's ability to retain a comfortable state of mind although experiencing the infant's feelings' (1959: 105). The infant's envy then distorts her capacity for receiving projections into a greedy devouring of his psyche, and he misrepresents her balanced outlook as indifference.

So far I have outlined Bion's hypothesis of a pathological matrix of adverse endowment with adverse nurture, which leads to the forming of a psychotic personality at the outset of life. From then on there will be an ever-widening divergence between the psychotic and the non-psychotic parts of his personality, and Bion thinks that we will not understand psychosis until we recognize this. In that part of the personality which is psychotic (which to a greater or lesser degree is in everybody) the mind is neither thinking nor perceiving. Through the processes described the psyche has been altered. The objects it now desires and which it will experience as good are those which assist the process of expulsion. Bion sums it up:

> The model I propose for this development is a psyche that operates on the principle that evacuation of a bad breast is synonymous with obtaining sustenance from a good breast. The end result is that all thoughts are treated as if they were indistinguishable from bad internal objects; the appropriate machinery is felt to be, not an apparatus for thinking the thoughts but an apparatus for ridding the psyche of accumulations of bad internal objects.
>
> (Bion 1962a: 112)

Once the psyche is no longer a thinking, perceiving mind, it uses projective identification not only excessively, which it does, but also differently. Instead of being used for normal communications with objects, as when a normal infant cries to and for its mother, projections are used to evacuate and to eradicate the awareness of the self and the object. They are loaded with enormous hostility; they are weapons – boomerangs which destroy the foundations for intuitive knowledge of the self and object. In such a psyche, impressions from within or without cannot be converted into the type of elements normally in the mind, which can then be repressed, or be dream-thoughts, or be conscious, or unconscious, and allow a state of being awake and being asleep. In the non-psychotic part of the personality, perceptions, a delusion, a dream, or a phantasy, are what they are partly through contrast with one another. In psychosis these mental differentiations do not form and all elements have equal value. All are the same and one is as real or unreal as another. Nor is there depth to the mind. Items are spread out, flat, or in some other shape. Of course, a psychotic patient has been taught and he knows words like 'being awake', 'delusion', but in so far as the use emanates from his psychotic self, they refer to phenomena which are different from the normal.

The world in which the psychotic exists has also departed from the ordinary. It is more bizarre even than the primitive world of part-objects full of projections, which Melanie Klein described as the universe of the normal paranoid-schizoid position. The difference is due to the sadistic splitting attacks on eyes, ears, indeed on all organs of awareness, and the hatred with which the fragments are projected, in Bion's phrase,

> to penetrate or invest their object. In the patient's phantasy the expelled parts of ego lead an independent and uncontrolled existence, either contained by or containing the external objects; they continue to exercise their function as if the ordeal to which they have been subjected had served only to increase their number and provoke their hostility to the psyche which ejected them. In consequence the patient feels himself to be surrounded by bizarre objects.
>
> (Bion 1957: 47)

Bion gives examples:

> If the piece of personality is concerned with sight, the gramophone when played is felt to be watching the patient; if with hearing, then the gramophone when played is felt to be listening to the patient. The object, angered by being engulfed, swells up, so to speak, and suffuses and controls the piece of personality that engulfs it: to that extent the particle of personality has become a thing.
>
> (Bion 1957: 51)

And he concludes: 'The consequences for the patient are now that he moves, not in a world of dreams, but in a world of objects which are ordinarily the furniture of dreams' (Bion 1957: 51).

Moreover, because frustration is intolerable and all frustration involves waiting in time and finding in space, space and time too are destroyed and do not exist. In such a universe it is always now, and self and object become increasingly bizarrely confused. The psychotic feels that his ego and his object are incurable, and that his psychotic state of mind is a prison from which he has no means of escape.

At this point I would like to offer an illustration of psychotic functioning by describing a few events in the analysis of a five-year-old boy, Matthew. I told him that there was a Whit Monday coming and there would be no session on that Monday. Matthew arrived for a following session with a black and red bruised eye, a most shocking sight. He desperately needed comfort but could only scream, cough, and spit.

The next day began with an improbable attempt at seduction. He pushed down his trousers, showed me his bottom for a moment, confusedly calling it 'my wet po po' with a gesture of 'You like this'. Then he was as the day before, crying, screaming, shouting for his mother, coughing, and spitting. In among his screams I heard the word 'five'. I said the four days next week were a shocking hurt to him. Matthew cut in shouting and crying, 'Not four, three times, five, not seven, not four, seven'. He screamed even more piercingly. I thought the whole house and all the neighbours must be hearing him. His distress was enormous, or, rather, my feeling of his distress and also my disgrace with the neighbours were enormous. At one moment Matthew screamed and said, 'I am going to come right near you and make you stop, stop, stop talking!', and he pressed himself on me. I made one or two interpretations which just made him scream more. But then, when I interpreted that with his screams he felt he was getting bad tearing pieces out of himself and into me, there was a dramatic change. He was quiet. He became abstracted, twiddled his hair in his fingers, and touched various places on his head. He held his fingers near to his face and gazed at them minutely and fixedly for a long while. He then looked out of the window at the road below and said in a shaky but ordinary, very depressed little voice, 'Cars. A brown car, a blue car, a white car, a car with a sunroof. Not all cars have sunroofs', as if chatting to me. He altered again. He began repeating, 'Twit to whoo, twit to whoo'. I questioned him and he made a frame round each eye with his fingers and peered through it. He was still saying 'Twit to whoo' which slowly became 'Two it too, do it to, do it, do it, do it, do it', insistently and excitedly. He clutched his penis. I said that he felt that his eyes were in an owl, the night bird, seeing sex on Whit Monday and he couldn't bear waiting to see it and wanted sex to happen now. Matthew agreed, very excited. Then he asked me anxiously, 'Is there more time?' He took several pencils out of his box and said, now in a lady's anxious voice, 'Oh, my nerves, my nerves'.

He tried to keep the pencils bound in one bundle by tying them round with a bit of string to stop them falling apart. I said that he was trying to help himself, me, and his mother, all of us, he felt, ladies falling to pieces. He said, 'My pencils are in a mirror box at home.' It was almost the session's end. 'I'm going to make yellow butter. I must have a yellow bowl the same colour as the butter.' He rapidly found paints, yellow bowl and water, and stirred a yellow mixture quickly very smooth. He was shaky, but in control of himself.

Matthew's departure from the normal is tragically evident. The cancelled session on Whit Monday is completely intolerable to him. He cannot and will not bear it. The no-session is experienced by him concretely as sexual intercourse which is a physical blow to his eye. There is no time – it is not next week, but now. Nor is there space – his eyes, projected in phantasy into a night owl, are at the sex. Eyes out of his head, his mind feels like a head pierced by tearing pieces, and then, when relieved, is empty and still.

Matthew is full of hatred. After I said four days were a shock to him, he rages at the 'four'. 'Not four, three times. Five, not seven. Not four, seven', he screams. His greedy demand is for seven, for no frustration at all. He and his objects are smashed to pieces. He said, you remember, 'I am going to come right near you and make you stop, stop, stop talking!' His states are split, without links, merely successive, whether his head is tormented, or he is the owl, the anguished lady, or looking through the window at the cars. All had to him the same reality or unreality. There are bizarre formations, the most striking being his damaged eyes in the owl and the Whit Monday in the twit-to-whoo call. He is confused with all his objects. He is the owl, he is the anguished lady, even his bottom is mixed up with a po po, his word for his chamber pot.

As to the therapeutic interaction, I felt shattered by his screams, ruined in the eyes or ears of the household or neighbours, wrong in my approach to him, and, if right momentarily, soon wiped out, exactly, I suspect, as his mother felt. It is significant that the only interpretation which helped Matthew was the one about screaming piercing pieces out of himself into me. That is, only when I had experienced emotionally his enormous persecution and could verbalize that he was trying to evacuate bad fragments from his head, was I, for him, a good object. He was then quiet and still for a short time and could look out at the ordinary world, shaky, depressed, but with normal, if remote, perception of differences restored to him. He saw the different colours and noticed that not all cars have sunroofs.

However, his projective identification with a perceptive object is not retained. Before he goes, hatred and intolerance of separateness supervene. He annihilates colour differences, the perception of which had come at the only moment when he felt I understood him. He makes 'yellow butter', pulverizing any remaining gritty fragments: all is the same, no object relation is left.

The difficulty of working with Matthew is evident. Only one interpretation reached and changed him. I think, though some may disagree with this, that it is important to get to where the projected parts of his personality are located – for example, to where the owl is, seeing sex – to be with him, even if he misunderstands me in this instance as my being excited and therefore sexually stimulating to him. I think, or I hope, that he will even so feel a little less isolated. Mostly, however, I have to say that his psychotic process proliferates too fast for even this minimal contact to remain.

I find Bion's theories of enormous help in the struggle to find a way of working with a patient like Matthew. Much of such an analysis remains obscure and very uncertain in all ways. Before I discuss the question of the analytic treatment of psychosis, I want to quote Bion's description of a malignant figure which he thinks is characteristically resident in the inner world of the psychotic and which affects the therapeutic outcome. We return to the adverse matrix of mother and child, the matrix too, I think, for Matthew and his mother. Bion writes:

> If the mother cannot tolerate ... projections the infant is reduced to continued projective identification carried out with increasing force and frequency. The increased force seems to denude the projection of a penumbra of meaning. Re-introjection is effected with similar force and frequency. Deducing the patient's feelings from his behaviour in the consulting room and using the deductions to form a model, the infant of my model does not behave in a way that I ordinarily expect of an adult who is thinking. It behaves as if it felt that an internal object has been built up but has the characteristics of a greedy vagina-like 'breast' that strips of its goodness all that the infant receives or gives leaving only degenerate objects. This internal object starves its host of all understanding that is made available. In analysis such a patient seems unable to gain from his environment and therefore from his analysis.
>
> (Bion 1962a: 115)

The prospects for treatment, given all this, cannot be propitious, and yet in Bion's view, and that of many analysts, psychoanalytic treatment is relevant and possible. Anyone who has tried to work with a psychotic personality knows the anxiety and invasiveness which must be expected and carried by the therapist. We can all be fortified by

Bion's opinion that these are not necessarily due to our bad work, but are inescapable if we are doing our work, as is the obscurity of many of the patients' communications and the amount of incomprehension we have to try to tolerate. A psychotic patient is instantly in a state of projective identification with his therapist and maintains this state tenaciously. He forms what Herbert Rosenfeld calls a 'transference psychosis' (Rosenfeld 1954: 117). Rosenfeld, of course, is the other psychoanalyst who developed the work of Klein to advance greatly our understanding of psychotic states, but in this chapter I focus on features of the therapeutic process which can be understood more directly through Bion's work.

During treatment the patient's projections into the therapist, the room, and elsewhere construct a bizarre environment which, from fear and hostility, he tries to keep secret. He relies on his therapist to exercise the functions he has ejected and is still devoted to destroying. Under the load of anxiety and the barrage of splintered hostile projections, the therapist has to find a way of working, while meeting constantly the kind of ego-destructive internal object in the patient Bion described. The analyst or therapist also has to remember that, as a transference object, from the patient's point of view he is most of the time part of some split or bizarre formation. Also manifest in the transference is the patient's desperate need to get relief, which I think we saw with Matthew, and his hope of a cure. The problems which face him are vast: his ego and his internal objects are splintered and projected into various objects and lie in confusion in the psychic, organic, and physical world. Given his present condition and his adverse disposition, the therapeutic process will inevitably, I think, be far more distressing for him than for a more normal patient.

Bion points out that the psychotic patient who is able to attend for therapy will have also a non-psychotic personality, and this is, for us, a gain. He contends that, provided we recognize and analyse the abnormal functioning of the psychotic personality when it is operative, something worthy of the name of progress can take place. Though again, and I think that this is one of his most important contentions, such progress differs from the progress of the more usual patient. He describes it in the following way. If the patient's projections are received and understood, he may begin to feel less isolated and persecuted and his splitting may lessen. This may lead to an attempt to think, which is an essential part of the repair of his ego. This involves permitting entry to perceptions and projected bits, a process often experienced as an assault: the patient feels struck in the eye, or jabbed elsewhere, twitches, or may get a headache. Return of some awareness brings a new condition internally and externally. Internally, among

97

other figures, there is his ego-destructive superego, more menacing now because internal and also because less splintered and more whole. Externally the patient now faces his neurotic conflict, and, although he feels more human and more real, his inordinate superego anxiety and his intolerable conflicts with his objects will again drive him to free himself from psychic reality by splitting and projecting all means of awareness. That again will bring anxieties about insanity, a state which he will try to evade and to conceal. Then he will be driven once more to attempt to repair his ego, and return to reality and neurosis. Such is Bion's illuminating description of a forward movement to an aberrant depressive position which then impels retreat to the aberrant paranoid-schizoid position characteristic of the psychotic person. Bion thinks that such shifting back and forth can gradually lead to the patient sustaining a more human contact with whole objects and an increased ability to think and use verbal thought in place of action and projective identification. He stresses that the foundation of any improvement is the patient's own recognition of his psychosis: once he gains insight into the fact that he is ill he may begin to get well.

Although the difference between psychotic and non-psychotic functioning is so total, it can in practice be difficult to detect. I would like to illustrate this difficulty by describing another patient, Mrs L, whose material shows how easy it is to mistake psychotic functioning for normal.

Mrs L is a patient who has struggled with a large, often dominant, psychotic area in her personality. For the past few weeks she had been feeling less confused and frightened and less incapacitated. She has had no occupation for a long time, and once or twice recently she wondered during her sessions what she could think of doing now. She also told me that because she was feeling better her husband was going away for a fortnight. She feared this, thought it cruel, but felt she should accept it because he had stayed with her during the period when she was unable to be alone. I want to describe some events in a recent Friday session, the day after her husband left.

Mrs L arrived bleak, low in self-esteem, and very anxious. She spoke for a while, and when I interpreted that she felt very anxious because of a weekend with no sessions, alone in her house, a prey to strange figures and thoughts, she said, much moved, 'Of course'. Then she referred to various lectures she had been to in the past week. After that Mrs L said, 'I attended a lecture at the National Gallery this morning. I even asked a question.' She added doubtfully, 'It seemed all right. The question was a simple one, although the lecturer didn't know the answer. He thought it was thirteenth century, but he was at least one hundred years out.' Then very contemptuously: 'Anyone with any

98

general knowledge should know that! How can someone lecture and know so little? The lecturer had a speech defect. I, of course, have never had any of these little sinecures like teaching at the National Gallery. I have no need financially, of course, though I do have wide knowledge.'

By this time Mrs L was sounding 'big', and my thoughts were something like this: from past sessions I knew she thought I had defects both of accent and enunciation. She had also told me recently that it was evident that I knew nothing of literature, history, or the arts generally. Because of her repeated mention of lectures I found myself wondering if she had perhaps seen a poster advertising a lecture I was to give, and was feeling that if *I* could, surely *she* could be a lecturer and an analyst. Such were my thoughts, and at the same time I felt very unsure about what to make of Mrs L's communications. I was anxious, and I felt I must try to understand them, and must not just ignore them. So I said, 'You feel big in comparison to me who seems small, and as I, with my defects, am an analyst who has patients and gives talks, you feel you could.' Mrs L said: 'I agree with you about the big and the small. I am very big compared to you.' She spoke in a tone of stating an evident fact. Then, in a most pleased voice, as if I had showered her with compliments, she said, 'I think I could do it! But really I wouldn't like to be an analyst.' She continued in the manner of one refusing a gratifying invitation. I said, 'You heard me as inviting you to be an analyst, rather than that I was speaking of your feelings and phantasies.' Mrs L answered me, totally bewildered, 'But I don't have feelings and phantasies.' She repeated angrily, 'I don't have phantasies,' and then, very anxious, she withdrew from me and spoke coldly of entirely other things.

Quite evidently I had misunderstood and distressed my patient. She is bewildered, angry, cold, frightened, and she has to correct me. She tells me that she does not have phantasies. What then does she have? And how have I gone wrong? When she said, 'I don't have phantasies', what does she mean? I think she means what she said. Phantasies imply a distinction between real and unreal, between a wish and its fulfilment. She knows she is not functioning in that ordinary mode at that moment. Really, she had already given an indication of this when she agreed with me that she was big and I was small, and spoke as if these sizes were fact. I think here we capture a glimpse of the occurrence of the process Bion calls 'transformation in hallucinosis' (1965: 137–46).

The situation Mrs L dreads of being alone on the weekend and being unable to hold on to her mental improvement is already occurring in the session. She is reverting to abnormal modes of functioning as psychotic panic threatens. As a defence against the panic she starts to expand and to use her sense organs as apertures through which to squeeze, diminish, and then evacuate persecuting feelings and objects. In the end Mrs L has 'made' her persecutor into a small object outside of herself, which is then the analyst. This process of hallucinosis makes my smallness and her bigness a fact in her bizarre world.

Mrs L belongs to a particular group of patients described by Bion who cannot bear the dominance of the reality principle, but who do not completely evade frustration either. He thinks such a patient finds a resort in omniscience. Mrs L feels she has wide knowledge and moral superiority – she would not treat a patient the way I do. In this condition, she wants objects primarily for purposes of projective identification, that is, to be in, in order to cure herself, and when I said that she, not me, should be the analyst, she heard me as issuing an invitation, inviting her into me. My saying afterwards that this was only her phantasy was from her point of view a sudden horrifying ejection. She felt sadistically played with, seduced in and treacherously thrown out. For her psychotic self I think that it is even worse. Being an analyst was not a phantasy, as she said, it was a delusion which gave her at that moment an identity. It contained and repaired her dispersing personality, so that when I said it was her phantasy, I think she felt I was smashing bits of her repaired ego.

Now, why did I blunder so? One thing I did wrong was to attend to her words only and ignore what Mrs L had transmitted by projective identification. Had I instead given the priority to her projective identification, the whole situation would have looked rather different. My counter-transference, you will remember, was that I felt anxious and uncertain of what it all meant, did not know what to say, yet felt that I must try to make something of it. I think Mrs L was communicating exactly this: that she must try to manage, even though she feels anxious and very uncertain that mentally she will stay well enough. She feels she must try very hard. And she *is* trying hard. She managed to go to a lecture that morning, and she even asked a question. She was moved, you will remember, at the beginning of the session, when I understood her dread of the weekend, and had I continued with this theme I might have kept contact with her, but as it was I lost her. She very much wanted to negotiate the weekend without analysis as an ordinary patient would, but she feared that waiting for Monday was going to be intolerable. Internally, her conception of me as benign is disappearing: I am seen as defective because I know her needs and dreads and yet persist in leaving her. Thus accused, I am destroyed as a good object, as I suspect her husband is too. Thus internally she is alone with persecutors. As she talks, Mrs L only partially uses verbal thought. She also uses words to disperse her ego and to escape contact with objects and feelings too persecuting and too full of dread to be borne. This mixture of psychotic and normal is part of what made it difficult for me. When I failed to understand and analyse any of this, I was actually a defective analyst.

The blunders were mine, but one further factor of great importance was that Mrs L meant me to blunder. She was speaking to communicate and disperse anxiety, and simultaneously speaking with great, if very quiet, hatred, to mislead. She used our shared knowledge of what had transpired previously about her longing to work, about my defective accent and so on, to control my attention. She led me away from the acute anxiety roused by her ego-destructive superego saying to her that she is no better, that she is incurable, that she will not manage the weekend. Perhaps too I found it easier to attend to her neurotic conflicts about working than to face how fragile her ego still is, and how, under pressure, psychotic functioning becomes dominant.

To return to the session: the situation was that Mrs L had withdrawn from an analyst who was out of contact with her, a defective and highly persecuting object, and I had to try to work from there. However, in my own time afterwards, what Bion has called the analyst's later 'reverie', I tried to reflect on how and what had gone wrong, much as I have done here. This case of Mrs L illustrates some of the characteristic shifts and extreme conflicts and anxieties which face a patient, and the difficulties which confront and confuse an analyst, when a patient with a psychosis is making progress.

Bion's new conceptions of psychosis have made it more possible, I think, to work with patients like Mrs L, and even Matthew, who is more ill than Mrs L. In brief, Bion's theory is that in psychotic states there is overall divergence from the normal due both to what the mind has lost – the power of thinking, the capacity for awareness, sense organs for perceptions, mental depth and contrast – and to what the mind has become – fragmented, its elements concrete and without variety, its sense organs become apertures, its chief functions splitting and evacuating of bad fragments, an abnormal projective process which makes the world bizarre.

These are Bion's ideas. For me they are that truly rare thing – new scientific ideas. They have thrown light on the obscure territory of psychosis, and they will, I feel sure, illuminate it still further in the future.

8

Keeping things in mind

RONALD BRITTON

This chapter is about Wilfred Bion's concept of the 'container' and the 'contained'. He derived this notion from his clinical work, particularly with psychotic and borderline psychotic patients, and applied it in a very general way to individual and group behaviour. I want to approach my discussion of his concept through its clinical manifestations in analysis, and I will begin with a description of a patient who resembles those who provoked the idea in Bion's mind.

Miss A, as I shall call my patient, was compelled by threats from within herself to empty out her mind of the thoughts she was having. This she did by repeatedly flushing them down the lavatory. (This patient is also described above in Chapter 3.) There were days when she did this so often that she broke the mechanism. By the time she would tell me about this in her session she no longer knew what these thoughts were. The process, however, of emptying out was so severe that she felt empty of any ideas and any mental life; she complained of feeling 'unreal'. The quality the outside world acquired in this process was a sense of menace. As a consequence of this mental evacuation of 'something bad', she found it impossible to travel outside an imaginary boundary, which roughly coincided with the outskirts of London where she lived. Thus she was menaced from within by an inner presence or from without by unspecified dangers. If she took things in and held them in her mind she was in danger; if she expelled them from her mind she produced a menacing outside world. She could neither introject nor project without producing a fearful situation.

Her dilemma was epitomized in a memory she had of an experience she had had during the Second World War, which she often repeated to me; it functioned as a sort of paradigm, or, as Bion might have said, 'a configuration'. It was what Freud called a 'screen memory'; that is, it was a condensation of experience which functioned as an expression

102

of earlier unconscious memories, and a prototype for later experiences. In this memory she was an adolescent in a public air-raid shelter during a bombing attack. She felt overwhelmed and suffocated in the shelter where she was with her mother whose clinging anxiety oppressed her. She felt very urgently that she must get out. At the threshold she was terrified as she saw the bombs falling, and the street on fire. An air-raid warden confronted her in the entrance and told her not to leave. The conflict was intense and apparently unresolvable. She collapsed in the doorway, retaining consciousness but becoming paralysed, mute, and entirely without bodily sensations, so that she could not feel the pins which the examining doctors stuck into her to see if she could feel. It is this state of anaesthesia which has been used as a threat forever after, compelling her to perform compulsively her irrational activities. 'If you don't, you will get the feelings,' her internal voice said; so the 'feelings' which she so dreaded were the experience of having no sensations, for which reason she could never allow herself to have any local anaes-thetic, and endured any amount of dental pain, either at home or in the dental chair, to avoid it.

The threshold remained a crucial place materially and symbolically for her, and when she embarked for her sessions with me she would go in and out of her flat, which she shared with her mother, before she could finally leave and continue her journey to come and see me. This 'doing' and 'undoing' was to ensure that she did not bring the 'wrong ideas' with her from the flat. It was as if the ideas had to be encapsulated in the ritual of going in and out which she provided for herself and which she used to convey them to me. All that remained of the thoughts on finally crossing the threshold was the knowledge that they were 'bad'. They were now encapsulated in a designation that had no content and they were encapsulated by the ritual. What she sought from me were basically two things. One was to find sanctuary, and the other was to find meaning. She found sanctuary the moment she was under my roof. Once she was in the waiting room, and she always came a little early, she felt free of what she called 'the noise in her mind'. Once she was in the session, she would seek meaning, reiterating, 'What does it mean? What does it mean?'

Sanctuary seemed to be a sense of being in a safe place, which itself expresses an idea of being inside something good. Winnicott called this 'a sense of being held' (Winnicott 1960). Esther Bick equated it with having a sense of envelopment like a skin around oneself which protects and enfolds (Bick 1968). This idea has also been developed recently by Anzieu (1989). Bion himself referred to a mental skin (unpublished paper). The other element that she sought was *meaning*. This was felt by my patient to be something which would provide a desperately needed internal coherence to her thoughts, whose disconnectedness persecuted her. Bick has suggested that a focus of perceptual experience may provide cohesion for the infant, whether it be a nipple in the mouth or an object of the eye. This might describe the forerunner to what my patient was constantly seeking in looking to me for a central explanatory idea.

If the first of these qualities, 'sanctuary' (that is, a sense of being inside something secure), is lost, the individual feels that they are 'falling forever', or as a patient of mine put it, 'that there is no floor to the world'. If the second of these qualities, inner meaning, is lost, a sense of internal incoherence and fragmentation is felt. My patient, Miss A, found both intolerably distressing. The first of these states, which I called 'sanctuary' for my patient, Bion said was provided by a 'container'. The second, a sense of coherence crystallized by an organizing central idea, or 'selected fact', he described as the 'contained'. The 'contained' gives meaning to the context which contains it. The 'container' on the other hand gives shape and secure boundaries to that which it enshrines (Bion 1962b).

The analytic situation could be described as endeavouring to provide both of these – a bounded world (the container) where meaning can be found (the contained). The 'container and the contained' are terms Bion used in 1962 in his book *Learning from Experience* (Bion 1962b). But the concept was developed earlier in a series of three papers: 'On arrogance', in 1958; 'Attacks on linking', in 1959; and 'A theory of thinking', in 1962 (Bion 1962a).

In the last of these papers he expounded his theories on the nature of thought and the capacity for thinking. This is a piece of major metapsychology, and I believe a notable contribution to psychoanalysis. It has shed new light not only on psychopathology, but has also furnished a new rationale for the efficacy of psychoanalysis; namely, his notion of the transformation of experience through the process of 'containment'.

Bion defines his terms in *Learning from Experience* as follows:

Melanie Klein has described an aspect of projective identification concerned with the modification of infantile fears; the infant projects a part of its psyche, namely its bad feelings into a good breast. Thence in due course they are removed and reintrojected. During their sojourn in the good breast they are felt to have been modified in such a way that the object that is reintrojected has become tolerable to the infant's psyche. From the above theory I shall abstract for use as a model the idea of a container into which an object is projected and the object that can be projected into the container; the latter I shall designate by the term contained.

(Bion 1962b: 90)

That was Bion's own definition. What he added to Melanie Klein's account of projective identification was the observation that projective identification was often not simply an omnipotent phantasy, as she described, but that the patient took steps to give effect to his phantasy (see also Chapter 5 of this volume) – for example, that it was not the patient who was afraid, angry, helpless, despairing, impotent, or whatever, but that it was the analyst who should experience himself in that way. This was effected by the evocation or provocation of such an experience for the analyst, by the patient's verbal and non-verbal behaviour. The second additional point that Bion made was that this was a repetition of a normal stage of development between mother and infant, providing a primitive method of communication which was the forerunner of thinking. The mother, if she was receptive to the infant's state of mind and capable of allowing it to be evoked in herself, could process it in such a way that in an identifiable form she could attend to it in the infant. In this way, something which in the infant was near-sensory and somatic was transformed into something more mental by the mother which could be used for thought or stored as memory. The most basic way of thinking these thoughts would be something like having a dream. The nearly sensory-somatic qualities Bion called 'Beta elements', and those which become more mental in character he called 'Alpha elements'. The process by which Beta was transformed into Alpha he regarded as fundamental in the production of thoughts, and, as its nature was unknown, he did not want to give the impression that it *was* known, he called it 'Alpha process'.

If this process badly misfires, then something like the state of mind of Miss A can result. I would like to return to that in order to illustrate what I have been describing in theory. If the elements of potential experience are unprocessed – that is, if they remain as Beta elements – they cannot be treated like ordinary thoughts but neither can they be treated as ordinary perceptions of the material world. They are on the boundary of somatic and psychic experience, of mental and physical. Miss A was consciously aware of them, she struggled to describe something which she regarded as mental and yet could only treat as physical; something which had mental status but could only be physically removed. She would say to me, 'I know it sounds mad, but I do feel that these terrible things in my mind should be cut out, if only somebody would do an operation.' Of the various forms of removal she had already resorted to, I have already referred to one; flushing the lavatory. Others were repeated hair washing; compulsive bathing; and repetitious disposal of rubbish. In a long history of psychological troubles, she had used different routes and locations for the disposal of these elements. Since she could not make them truly mental, she could not keep them in her mind in the sense that one might keep thoughts as conscious, preconscious, or unconscious.

Basically there are three spheres where these precursors of thought, Beta elements, might go out of the mind: firstly into the body; secondly into the perceptual sphere; and thirdly into the realms of action – that is, in other words, firstly into psychosomatic or hypo-chondriacal symptoms; secondly into perceptual hallucinations; or thirdly into action. Miss A had at different times used all three. She had suffered a good deal of psychosomatic ill-health; it seems likely that these unprocessed elements had been discharged through physical means into her body. Even more often she had suffered hypochon-driasis, a state in which the dis-ease, in her mind, had been projected into her mental image of her body as disease. At other times these elements were projected into the perceptual sphere so that she 'heard' or 'saw' things she knew were not there. These episodes frightened her and she described them as 'like having nightmares whilst still awake'.

Miss A functioned as though she lacked a process for producing something that could be kept in mind, and she also appeared to lack a mind that could keep things in it. Bion formulated the notion that 'thinking' is dependent on the successful outcome of two main mental developments. One is the development of thoughts; the second is development of the apparatus necessary to deal with the thoughts. Sometimes he called this the 'mental apparatus', sometimes simply 'thinking'. So, he argues, thinking comes about in order to deal with thoughts. Either of these two developments may go wrong. These capacities have their origins, as I have been saying, in the link between infant and mother in which knowledge develops. This knowledge he designated as the 'K' link, to distinguish it from the two other links between objects that he referred to, namely love, which he called the 'L' link, and hate, which he called the 'H' link. The origin of the K link was in the process between mother and child based on the infant's use of projective identification and the mother's capacity to receive it and modify it. The subsequent introjection by the child of an object based on this capacity of the mother provided the child with an internal object capable of knowing and informing. In other words, the person who internalizes such an object is capable of self-knowledge and communication between different aspects of themselves. They can experience themselves and think about themselves.

We might use Freud's terminology and say they have a helpful superego. What Bion suggested was that if this relationship between mother and infant goes badly wrong, instead of a helpful superego, an 'ego-destructive superego' develops. Normally, the integrative processes of the depressive position install within the personality a whole internal object, which can function as the ego or conscience. Instead, when containment goes wrong in some people it produces a part of themselves opposed to themselves – an 'ego-destructive superego' (Bion 1959: 107; 1962b: 96–7). For such a person integration therefore spells catastrophe. Miss A did not have a helpful superego. She had an internal object that forbade her to think and demanded that she rid herself of her thoughts.

Bion has suggested that a maternal object who failed to introject – that is, a mother who failed to absorb the infant's projections – was perceived by the child as hostile to any attempt at projective identification, or any attempt by the child to know the nature of its mother. The child had an idea, therefore, of a world that did not want to know it, and did not want to be known.

How this internal situation manifested itself in analysis was first described in his paper 'On arrogance', where he found the presence of a triad of arrogance, stupidity, and curiosity (Bion 1958). He felt that they indicated the presence of psychotic thinking as a consequence of what he called a 'primitive mental catastrophe'. The 'stupidity' was the manifestation of something obstructing that process of 'taking things in' which underlies communication. Familiarity with its operation has made it clear that this problem is something that crops up in many analyses, and not only as a major feature in severely disabled patients. It sometimes is felt to be in the analyst; sometimes in the patient; and sometimes in some other location altogether from which it intervenes to thwart understanding. If it is felt by the patient to be in the analyst in the form of complacency or arrogance, the analyst is thought to be impermeable to the reality of the patient. If it is active in the patient, the patient cannot 'take in' what the analyst is saying.

A patient considerably less disturbed, Mr B, said to me: 'The reason why I go on and on at you is that I must let you know how I feel. I don't feel I get it across to you by just saying it. I have to make you feel it. I don't think that you take it in.' How this obstructing force moves around within a session I can illustrate from another patient. This patient, a man, said: 'I am deaf in one ear today,' and then remained silent for some time. 'I feel thick-headed,' he then said. 'It's not going to be any good today,' he went on despondently. 'I won't be able to think. I feel muddle-headed.' As the session proceeded I sensed a quiet despair in my patient, and I thought to myself that he believed I did not want to know what he was thinking and feeling. So I put this to him. He said, 'Yes', very promptly, and he went on to say, 'You must be feeling impatient, waiting for me to get on with this analysis. But I feel muddled, unclear about anything, stuck.' In contrast to him he believed that I already knew what he should do; already knew what was in his mind, and knew what it all meant. All I knew in reality, however, was that my patient felt he could not enlighten me about himself. When eventually he did begin to talk he did so in an unusual way; its effect on me was that I could not remember clearly what he said, I was unable to make anything of it. I felt muddleheaded, stupid, and impatient with myself. I blamed myself, and I tried to think about the sense of impatience I had with myself. Then I realized that I was imagining privately that other colleagues, whose abilities I admired, would know with crystal clarity what the meaning was of what was being said. It was only then that it occurred to me that this was the internal situation that my patient had brought with him. He had arrived to talk to an analyst who, he imagined, did not know what it felt like to be ignorant, and in comparison with whom he felt ignorant.

Once the preliminary work of the session had been done, he had begun to communicate this state of mind to me, not in words but by projective identification. So I said to him that his words today gave me a sense of what it was like to feel muddled and unsure of what was happening, in contrast to an imaginary superior person like myself who, he thought, always knew what was happening. He reiterated that he felt that there was something that he ought to know and did not know which I would expect him to know. It was only then that I remembered that shortly before I had told him that I would not be working on a particular day a few weeks thence. It occurred to me that he felt ignorant about my activities outside the sessions. This for my patient reactivated a lurking sense of inferiority which he always felt about any activities of mine, which, like his parents' sexual life together, when he was a small child, was beyond his comprehension. He appeared to experience it as a form of exclusion which condemned him to a shameful exposure of inferiority.

The belief that they are dealing with an impermeable object coated with an impregnable sense of superiority drives some personalities to violence. It underlies a good many of the situations of spiralling violence which occur in professional situations, whether in psychiatry, or social work, or teaching, or in psychoanalysis. If the patient, client, child, or someone else feels that they cannot 'get through', that they are making no impact or impression on the person whom they are addressing, then an intensification may occur in their efforts to project and enforce feelings within the professional recipient. This often produces a vicious circle, since we are all apt to respond to this by 'hardening' inside. We may communicate this hardening up in our choice of words, in our expression, or in our tone of voice; this, in turn, provokes more efforts to intrude forcibly. In other people or at other times, the sense of being faced with an impervious object induces an acquiescent despair; this was so in the patient to whom I have just been referring.

Fear of the containing object does not only take the form of a fear of being denied access, ingress, or acceptance. Another fear results from a phantasy of the projected self being taken in and then destroyed, a fear that one's nature is taken in by the other's devouring curiosity and somehow lost in the process; that one is comprehended but nullified during the process. It is not an uncommon fear that analysis will strip the individual of his individuality, or that particular gifts will be lost, but in severe forms this idea can lead to profound fears of a psychotic kind, as in my patient Miss A. She feared entombment whilst still alive. One version of this was her fear that she would be buried alive; incarcerated in a coffin, unable to speak or move, she feared that she would then be buried. It was one of several versions of a configuration that haunted her, in all of which she would be enclosed, confined, and denuded of life. As a small child, one form this had taken was a phantasy she had of being trapped in 'a tube' inside her mother. Her mother, in fact, did have a tubal pregnancy. She had heard a lot of conversation about this and it was for this reason that her mother was hospitalized. This image gave shape to already existing phantasies which derived from early infantile experiences with her mother. She grasped as a little girl that this tubal relationship meant death for one or the other party, mother or baby. She repeated this fear symbolically in her treatment with me. There were times when she became afraid that I would listen to what she said, take it in, and then I would tell her that it meant nothing, literally nothing. Or that I would tell her that it added up to nothing, that it made no sense. This would have meant she was mad. A related fear was that I would take in what she said and forget it. This was a cause of great panic because she could not remember things once she had told them to me, and thus feared that they would be lost completely. She constantly tried to retrieve her memories from my mind.

Although I have used these patients, Miss A and Mr B, to illustrate the process designated by Bion as 'containment', the difference between them was great. To speculate as to the differences, I need to refer to Bion's own theories of the origin of these problems between infant and mother and their sequel in the individual. He suggested that on the one hand there was the patient's inborn disposition to excessive destructiveness, hatred, and envy; on the other, there was the environment which denies to the patient the use of mechanisms of splitting and projective identification. 'On some occasions', he wrote, 'the destructive attacks on the link between patient and environment, or between different aspects of the patient's personality, have their origin in the patient, in others in the mother' (Bion 1959: 106).

In the case of psychosis he thinks that there is always a significant innate contribution from the infant. In particular he suggested that some personalities could not tolerate the capacity of the mother to contain experiences which they themselves could not, and that this provoked envious attacks. This formulation was based on his analytic work with some psychotic and borderline patients, whom he found could not bear the analyst's ability to remain balanced when subjected to these projections.

I have suggested elsewhere (Britton *et al.* 1989) that there is a third influence; that is, the identity and personality of the other member of the early Oedipal situation, namely the father. This was very different in the childhood experience of the two patients I have described. Miss A's father was psychotic and hostile to the precarious relationship between her and her mother. Mr B's father was solicitous and provided support in the early difficulties he and his mother experienced together. Father's capacity to contain his wife's anxiety probably enabled her to be more receptive and internally free than she otherwise would have been to respond to her infant's emotional states.

In addition to this indirect effect, I think that there is another way in which father influences these developments for good or ill, in that he acts as a figure for identification and thus becomes an internal object capable of giving help or sabotage to the nursing couple as the case may be. In the case of Miss A it was sabotage, and that was what it felt like in her treatment. On the large scale this took the form of negative therapeutic reactions, by which I mean an adverse response to any progress. On a small scale it was evident in outbreaks of intrusive interruptions in her thinking when we had finally begun to communicate in the sessions.

The analysis of Mr B was very different in that it was much easier for him to make use of the analytic situation. I have noticed that, where the problem has its roots mainly in maternal difficulties of containment, the patient is often very responsive to the kind of analytic approach described here and in the previous chapter by Mrs O'Shaughnessy. However, I find that such patients are markedly dependent on the analytic process itself, and are very vulnerable to interruptions such as those caused by breaks and are particularly prone, I find, to lose their functional capacities during breaks. But I am convinced that the difference in severity between Miss A and Mr B that I have illustrated is not simply a reflection of the degree of parental psychopathology. In severe cases I think that innate factors play a significant role. In Miss A, for example, her father's mad destructiveness provided an external location for her own conspicuous envious and nihilistic trends, as a result of which there was, by projective identification, a fusion between that hostile aspect of herself and her perception of her father's hostility. This introduced into her personality what I have called an 'Alien Object' (Britton 1986), which she experienced as both part of herself and not part of herself. In fact she used to say, 'It must be me but it doesn't feel like me.' This enabled her to exonerate her mother from any attribution of malignancy as she split this off from her mother, attached it to her idea of her father, and cemented it there with her own projected hostility. Her mother was consequently internally represented as inadequate and restricted, a lifeless object in which she felt entombed. Her father was perceived as unrestrained, totally free, and dangerous; a picture of uncontained violence, who destroyed any relationship he entered, just as my patient envisaged him destroying the peace of her childhood home. The air-raid shelter memory, functioning as a condensation in the way that a dream-image might do, could be seen as a representation of the alternatives of a confining mother, and, outside that relationship, an attacking father with his bombshell curses and angry words which she could not keep out of her mind. Here we have the image of the claustrophobic–agoraphobic dilemma, which Henri Rey (1979) pointed out is characteristic of the borderline phenomenon, a deathly container, or exposure in a shattered world.

Bion, as I said earlier in this chapter, applied this basic relationship of the container to the contained in a very general way to individual and group relationships. He saw it as a pre-determined form (a pre-conception) which would seek its first expression in the mother–infant relationship. Whatever phantasies it engendered in that early encounter would shape for the individual fundamentally his expectations in all subsequent situations and also in his relationship with himself; that is 'inside himself', as we often put it. This theory implies that in our phantasies of our own self-composition we see ourselves sometimes as containing vital things, such as vital organs or other vital components, or at other times we see ourselves as inhabitants of our bodies. In older language we might have said that sometimes we see ourselves as bodies containing our souls, and at others as souls confined within our bodies.

Bion, in a description of the 'container' in an unpublished paper entitled 'Catastrophic change' (1967), says that 'some aspect of the personality is stable and constant, and that this is maintained as the only force likely to contain emergent ideas which express new awareness of

111

reality of the self or the world.' If the relationship between this continuous self and the recurrently changing emergent self is mutually enhancing, development takes place. This relationship he describes as 'symbiotic'. If, however, that continuous identity which he called 'the container' is disrupted by new self-development or new self-discoveries, then psychic change is experienced as catastrophic, since the changes disintegrate the sense of self-continuity. When this happens the subjective experience is one of fragmentation. In these circumstances, in order to preserve a sense of continuity of existence, *all* change must be resisted and no new experience allowed to emerge. This mutually destructive relationship of container and contained Bion called 'parasitic'. I prefer to call it 'malignant containment'.

As I have described, faced with these two catastrophic alternatives, incarceration or fragmentation, some people, like my patient Miss A, remain paralysed at the frontier, on the threshold. If she left the shelter and confines of her already existing ideas about herself and her mother, which could not accommodate any growth, she thought that her world would be shattered and her continuous self annihilated. However, if she remained confined to her cramped, rigid view of her mother and herself, it meant the stifling of thought. I was to see this pattern repeating itself again and again as we tried to enlarge her view of things by the inclusion of new ideas within the context of her relationship with me, which took years to change.

This describes what we might call a 'persecutory view' of containment. There is of course a corresponding belief in its opposite – ideal containment; a belief that an absolute fit between container and contained should exist. In this, perfect understanding would be the order of the day, failing which a feeling of persecution would follow. Here I think that we see one of the innate factors in operation. In some personalities, small discrepancies in understanding, or between words and meaning, or between intention and execution, or interpretation and experience, or between ideal and real cannot be tolerated. The containment is exploded and meaning is in fragments.

If we are to live within ourselves or in our families or institutions, a degree of mutual recrimination between container and contained seems inevitable. Some amount of friction is, after all, part of life. I think this has been most eloquently expressed by the seventeenth-century metaphysical poet, Andrew Marvell, that most sensuous of Puritan poets. His poetic contribution to the relationship I have been describing follows the fashion of the late seventeenth century for literary debates between body and soul. What has been remarked on as unique, in addition to his wit, is the way Marvell 'avoids favouring one side or the other in the dispute, or resolving the problem of the mutual incompatibility of the participants' (Wilcher 1986: 219).

I will end by quoting from his even-handed 'Dialogue between the soul and body', and you will see what I mean about the mild mutual persecution. Soul begins by complaining of imprisonment within his mortal frame.

> O, who shall from this Dungeon raise
> A soul enslaved so many ways?
> With bolts of bones, that fettered stands
> In feet, and manacled in hands.
> Here blinded with an eye; and there
> Deaf with the drumming of an ear.

Body replies, complaining of the tyranny he suffers from this Soul, who, by breathing life into him, he says, 'Has made me live to let me die'. Soul's riposte is to grumble at the afflictions from Body of sensations of grief and pain. He says, 'I feel, that cannot feel, the pain.' Body, however, has the last word, and perhaps speaks for all of us, describing what it is to be afflicted with the qualities of psychic life, giving us a catalogue familiar to those who have suffered a touch of the depressive position. Body complains that thanks to his containing a Soul he suffers from hope, fear, love, hate, joy, sorrow, knowledge, memory:

> Whom first the cramp of hope does tear,
> And then the palsy shakes of fear;
> The pestilence of love does heat,
> Or hatred's hidden ulcer eat;
> Joy's cheerful madness does perplex,
> Or sorrow's other madness vex;
> Which knowledge forces me to know,
> And memory will not forgo;
> What but a soul could have the wit
> To build me up for sin so fit?

9

As if: the phenomenon of not learning

RUTH RIESENBERG MALCOLM

An earlier version of this chapter was given as a 'Bion Lecture'. The present version was given at the 36th International Psychoanalytical Congress at Rome in 1989 and subsequently published in the *International Journal of Psycho-Analysis* (1990) 71: 385–92.

I want to express my gratitude to Dr Hanna Segal for reading a draft of this chapter and making very helpful suggestions.

Analysis is a process which aims to achieve psychic change through understanding – that is, an emotional experience of learning.

It was Helen Deutsch who in 1942 coined the term 'as-if personality' to describe certain types of people about whom she says: 'The whole relation to life has something about it which is lacking in genuineness and yet outwardly it runs "as-if" it were complete.'

In this chapter I want to speak of the patient's 'as-if' response to analysis – a false connection with the analyst and the interpretations in the sessions, which gives an outward impression of understanding and progress, while in fact the whole process lacks something real, does not feel genuine, and seems to be going nowhere.

In most, if not all, analysis we can find the as-if behaviour in our patients, operating like any other defence or resistance against insight. But in some patients, this 'as-ifness', as behaviour in analysis, comes to constitute their basic mode of responding to the analyst's attempts to bring insight and change. This way of functioning aims at keeping an appearance of an analysis in progress, while the patient's main objective will be to keep the situation immobilized. A static stituation acts for these people as a kind of reassurance, a kind of proof that they are all right, do not need any change, which they prove by perceiving themselves endowed with keen analytic perceptions and gifts and rich emotions.

Many of these patients come to analysis for reasons that they find difficult to be precise about – a general malaise, some vague anxieties and discomfort; also on occasions the hope for some professional gain. The fact is that they are near breaking point, a fact more often than not unrecognized by them. I think they are patients who have barely managed to survive psychically, by maintaining a particular split in their personality. A vast area of fragmentation is encapsulated by a false structure.

Winnicott (1960) described very vividly the formulation of a 'false self' as a protection of a 'true self' that could not develop due to maternal failure. He says that in an early stage the infant is most of the time unintegrated and very rarely fully integrated. I would very much agree with Winnicott's description, but I would like to add that the infant, when not met by what he calls mother's 'devotion' and what I would tend to call mother's 'alpha function' (Bion 1962a), not only fails to integrate, but is also exposed to active processes of disintegration, derived from destructive as well as from defensive sources, which increase and complicate the unintegrated states, creating an abnormal development. As I said above, this results in fragmentation which becomes precariously enclosed in a false structure.

I think that this false structure is based on a falsely idealized object. It is doubly false, not only because excessive idealization falsifies, but also because of the object's own pathology.

The patient's equilibrium is threatened by life.

The state I am describing can be illustrated by the way patient B described herself in the preliminary interview. She wore a long knitted pullover, too big for her, and probably belonging to somebody else. It was scruffy and dirty, literally covered with holes, big and small. The patient spoke in a grandiose way of her ambitions and plans for her future work. While listening to her I kept asking myself, 'Are holes the substance of this garment, and will the wool hold them together?'

A common charactistic of these patients is the desperate need they seem to have to *agree* with what the analyst says: sometimes even disagreement gives the impression of being orchestrated to emphasize the points of agreement. They also often balance what the analyst says by interventions that maintain the equilibrium.

In these analyses many areas are apparently addressed by the analyst's interpreting and are furthered by the patient's associations – only for it eventually to be realized by the analyst that nothing has been achieved. The patient has learned a lot about 'psychoanalysis' but achieved no insight.

In this situation it appears that both patient and analyst are speaking the same language, meeting for the same reason; that is, to get analytic understanding. More often than not there would appear to be many points of agreement. The analyst believes he is doing analysis with the aim of furthering therapeutic insight. The patient behaves as if this were true. But actually he is coming to analysis, as I said before, for a different reason. His aim is precisely to avoid any emotional learning. I think that in fact those people feel hopeless of ever being understood, and they need to maintain a relationship with an object, the analyst, who is not expected, or allowed, to function. What he is expected to do is (omnipotently) to declare them 'well' and if possible make them into analysts or experts in analysis. Simultaneously, something called 'the analysis' is highly idealized and felt to be full of promise, and somehow expected to last for life.

In the 'as-if' analytical situation there are common traits in patients' reactions. They will often refer to what the analyst has interpreted in such general ways that the analyst gets very little information about what the patient did hear or understand. Common expressions are *'that'*, *'what you said'*, *'it'*, or *'what you think'*. Another common phenomenon is that these patients will often get hold of that bit of the analyst's wording that actually had been unnecessary, or was of very secondary importance, and will elaborate on that peripheral point, ignoring the important points.

On occasion, the patients report intense suffering, pain, or difficulties, but the analyst's feelings usually do not correspond to those reports, as they do with other patients. There is often an atmosphere of morality, and the analyst has vague feelings of guilt, sometimes mingled with irritation or despondency.

Bion used the expression 'reversible perspective' to describe this clinical situation. In the various chapters on this subject in *Elements of Psychoanalysis* (1963), he presents an inspiring clinical picture, which he examines in the light of his ideas on preconception–realization, minus L, H and K, the Oedipal myth; and he links the phenomenon predominantly to (unbearable?) pain. I will not review his ideas here, but I will draw from some of those which I feel to be directly pertinent to my subject.

In his description of 'reversible perspective' he compares it to the agreement two people would appear to have about the disposition of lines, light, and shade, but in those lines one sees a vase and the other sees two faces, yet they think they see the same thing. Bion says, 'the interpretation is accepted, but the *premises have been rejected*' (1963: 54, my italics). In my view this replacement is generally done by the patient very subtly shifting his focus: while stating his acceptance of the analyst's interpretation he has actually neutralized it or emptied it of substance. The result of this action is an accumulation of meaning-lessness.

I will present some material from several patients. Patient A is a headmaster in a secondary school. He is a very ill man in his sixth year of analysis. The example is from a session in which his behaviour was typical.

In the session, A was complaining about one thing and another. He had quarrelled with several people. He complained especially about Nancy, a teacher at his school, who did not support him when the situation at school was breaking down. My attempts to say something were brushed off. He seemed irritated by my speaking, while at the same time he seemed impatient to get something from me. He kept going back to Nancy and her lack of help. Finally I managed to say that I thought that something was going on which we did not seem to manage to grasp: that most of my attempts to say something were interrupted and discarded by him; and that his preventing me from talking must make him feel me to be unsupportive and unhelpful. I added that he was feeling pressured and angry, and feared he might break down with *me* not helping him.

A relaxed. His posture and manner changed; he became thoughtful; and after some moments he started speaking about one of his pupils who was under such pressure that he feared that he might have a mental breakdown. From this association onwards we seemed to get involved in a dialogue in which whatever I said, whether interpretation, elaboration of it, or just repetition of what I had said, was accepted, somehow agreed with, and immediately applied to one of his pupils and expanded in the context of that child's experience. Several times I tried to describe what was going on, and finally, when he once again said, 'It is like Peter...', I interrupted him and pointed out there and then what was happening. This time he managed to listen and take in what I said. I interpreted that this breaking the connections with me kept us immobilized and did *not* allow him to apply the understanding to himself. He interrupted me here, sounding very depressed, and said that what I was speaking about was schizophrenic thinking. My patient, up to a point, could get the gist of what I said, but, by transferring it to one of his students, kept some of the meaning of the interpretation but in such a way that what I said did not affect *him*, and the situation remained unchanged, while he believed himself to be very understanding.

Patient B, who could be called 'once upon a time', had some similarity with A, but here the focus moved not to other people but to situations from her past that my interpretations seemed to remind her of. Her most common phrase was 'It is like when...', and then she would expand on relations with aunts, grandparents, school, and so on, in a way which was appropriate, but useless analytically. These seemed to be displays of illustrations of my interventions. During this period, when I was trying to make her aware of what she was doing, she had the following dream.

She was going up a slope, which seemed to lead to something that could be an eating house, but when she arrived there was a small plateau that led immediately to a slope leading down and ending in the original place.

I will not go into details and associations to the dream, but there was some understanding between us that the main meaning of the dream was the realization of the static position created in the analysis; we go up and down — that is, nowhere. This in turn led us to further manoeuvres of the same kind; now we seemed to agree on the lack of movement, appeared to be analysing it — that is, talking about many kinds of expressions of static situations. In other words, the so-called agreement on a static situation simply replaced the 'It is like when...'.

This material shows that both patients heard and retained the gist of the interpretation. The meaning of the words was correctly grasped and remembered, the formal content apparently intact. Still something happened to make the interpretation useless and devitalized.

Bion thinks that in situations of 'reversible perspective' 'splitting had been arrested in a static pose'. I have already spoken of how those patients invest in a static situation. I differ from Bion in that I do not think that the splitting is arrested, but what happens is that a different type of splitting takes place. It would appear as if the interpretations are being cut or sliced longitudinally. Everything said by the analyst seems to be there, as if each segment had been photocopied and repeats itself, scattered among different situations and people. Each new situation reproduces the interpretation as a faint echo of itself. What has been taken away by this slicing is the actual specificity, the substance of the interpretation, which is meant to bring meaning for the patient. The slicing of the analyst's interpretations differs from a fragmentative type of splitting, and does arrest the latter, at least for the time being.

I have called this type of splitting 'slicing'. I have taken the word from a dream of a patient, C, which took place when I was trying to get some co-operation from her in facing the kind of situation I have been describing.

In the dream a woman was insisting that the patient should go to a patisserie. The patient, though liking sweets, did not particularly want to go, because she knew that the woman would force her to buy a cream bun, which she does like, but did not want to get because, for some reason, she knew that it was the woman who would enjoy the cream. Suddenly she saw in the shop that there was on display a beautifully, symmetrically cut cake, each slice so thin that no cream was noticeable.

In this patient's analysis, my interpretations, or parts of them, were repeated and displayed in her associations, but out of focus. This was done through slight, rather clever shifts. The impression in the session was of a great activity, giving the illusion of something continually happening, when actually from an analytic point of view the one and main thing that was happening was the neutralization and destruction of my work. As in my patient's dream, slicing is the solution. The woman will not get the cream, neither will the patient be affected. Nothing will change.

This common phenomenon I am describing often gives the analyst a curious feeling of hovering between thinking that the patient's action is voluntary or conscious or an unconscious bizarre behaviour and between the feeling that the patient is re-enacting something or that he is plainly lying.

The thin barrier between the levels in which the patient is functioning expresses the peculiar division of his personality which I described previously, the division that the as-if analysis helps to maintain. What happens is that it provides an artificial sense of wholeness, which is continually threatened by real and basic conflicts; by a terror of feelings of hopelessness in facing an internal world of disintegration, and objects felt as dead and beyond repair. The pull of the existing destructive impulses attacks any feeling of real relief and help from the analyst.

I will illustrate this with material from patient D. He is French, and has been coming for several years to analysis. He works in an international corporation and speaks several languages perfectly, including Spanish and English. The analysis was conducted in English. The patient often had to take short trips for his business.

During a period in the analysis in which there was the problem of having to make us equal, as well as the emergence of some real depression, he dreamed the following dream (this version of the dream, as well as the associations to it, is abridged):

In the dream he was in a party in a big house that belonged to some people called Corbeaux. He stopped to tell me that 'corbeau' meant raven. There were quite a number of people around and lots of things were going on. Mme Corbeaux started to show him around. The house was very luxurious. They stopped in a room that he found impressive. It had belonged to the au-pair girl who had left. The room was full of empty shells, on tables and shelves, and they were very pretty. But what was most impressive was that the floor was completely covered by them. He found it all quite disturbing and woke up.

He associated, rather fluently, to many things, but he kept coming again and again to the shell-covered room, and the strange effect it had on him. The subject of 'au pair' was a familiar one in the analysis, meaning literally that we were equals. I asked if he had any association to the shells. A bit shame-faced he said that it reminded him of his last trip to the Middle East. He went to the Dead Sea. There were many notices asking people not to remove shells, stones, or any other objects from the shore. He took several shells with him. After some more remarks about this, he told me that he was reminded of a saying in Spanish: '*Cria cuervos y te sacaran los ojos*' that, roughly translated, means 'Nurse ravens and they will pick your eyes out'.

I wish to show with this material how, when the patient feels his defences not functioning any more, he feels exposed to a situation he believes unfaceable.

Let us look first at his expression in the dream 'the au-pair girl who had left'. As I said before, during the time of the dream the subject of his and my being equals was very much in the foreground of the analytic work, and it was one of the ways he used to try to keep a balance to which the pair of us contributed, but to no avail. At this time in the analysis my interpretations had managed to touch him, and his sense of 'our equality' had left him.

Once this defence lost its effectivenesss he felt exposed to the sight of the state of his internal objects. Those, though idealized (the beautiful shells), were stolen, empty, and dead. In the analysis by his continuous use of as-if behaviour, the interpretations were appropriated and deadened by being emptied of meaning. They were robbed of their potential usefulness. His own association to the shells had to do with stealing them from the Dead Sea.

In the dream there was also an awareness of the shells being disturbing, and he was embarrassed and uncomfortable in telling me about his thieving. In this sense one can see that he was becoming aware not only of his state, but also of his own contribution to this. This incipient awareness was very disturbing for the patient.

Melanie Klein spoke about the difficulties that the baby experiences when it begins to integrate objects and self, with the ensuing awareness of psychic reality. John Steiner (1987) describes the specific difficulties of the transition from the paranoid-schizoid position to the depressive position. He refers to the intense anxieties and pain inherent in this transition, which on some occasions result in a compromise: a pathological organization, which perpetuates the vicious circle.

Coming back to D's material, he experienced this difficulty as an impossibility: he could not face his horror of and guilt for his internal world, created originally in his development. (I will not go into details of this, but I think that the 'Dead Sea' had to do with his mother, a very ill woman, and his own deadening impulses.) These feelings were made worse in the analysis by his continuous use of as-if behaviour. His solution then was to destroy my sight by plucking my eyes out.

After this dream there was a slight shift in the patient's attitude: his behaviour became a bit more genuine. This brought to the fore very intense anxieties which brought about other defences.

D had had on and off in the analysis problems of hearing. At first I did not know if he had a hearing impediment. I raised my voice and called this hearing problem to his attention. He had the problem investigated and the results were inconclusive; the word used by the ENT doctor was 'borderline'. During this time the hearing problems increased, and, since his attempts to prevent my seeing what was going on had failed, a new symptom emerged. He complained of having something like a fog in front of his eyes. Ophthalmological examinations were as inconclusive as the audiological ones. Another new symptom appeared: intense itching over his whole body, which prevented him from listening or thinking. The itching was sporadic and infrequent, while the seeing problem was of long duration.

The analysis during and after the dream period had brought the patient closer to perceiving problems which he felt as unbearable. This perception extended in some degree to the awareness of his use of reversible perspective, and the effects of this on the analysis. His dilemma was either to face and work through his problems, with all the horror, hatred, and pain involved in this, or to resort temporarily to different methods.

Bion says that when the patient cannot reverse perspective at once, he can resort to altering his perceptions, which could be seen as a delusional attempt to keep a static condition. He says that this temporary altering of perceptions is done in order to re-establish the operation of reversible perspective.

In D the three symptoms involved alteration of perception. The itching was an irritating distraction for him, and was temporary. But the problems of hearing and seeing were more serious, longer lasting, and potentially more damaging manoeuvres. They were destructive attacks on the perceptual apparatus itself, and their effects could result either in a shift back into reversible perspective or could bring further fragmentation and deterioration.

Patient D, in associating to the 'corbeau' dream, spoke about 'Ravens that pluck your eyes out', and some time after the dream, when some insight was achieved and he was aware that *my* vision of the situation was not impaired, he started *his* sight problem. This new symptom became an absorbing subject in the analysis, and it was extremely difficult to move beyond extended descriptions of his impaired sight and medical explorations, and his terror of blindness. As a result, the insight obtained up to the time of the onset of the symptom was blocked, and a new all-absorbing static situation established itself with great intensity. Due to this all my attempts to reach my patient were barred. This only diminished when the patient felt that he could re-establish his old methods of changing perspective. As can be seen, this attack on his perceptual apparatus brought a long cessation of the analytic work, and effectively destroyed the previous insight, therefore making any working through impossible.

In looking at the phenomena involved in 'reversible perspective' I think one can detect several elements at the root of it. In all the cases I have come across, certainly in the four mentioned in this chapter, I was struck by the balance between the maternal pathology and the patient's own envy. I will describe the latter under the heading of 'minus K'.

In his researches into learning, Bion picked up Klein's early and abandoned idea of an 'epistemophilic' instinct. He developed this idea by linking it to the operation of projective identification, which is for him the infant's first way of experiencing reality. Bion describes projective identification as the first link between baby and mother. The infant projects his feelings into his mother, who responds to them with what Bion called 'reverie', an activity which transforms the baby's raw sensations into tolerable feelings which can then be introjected. This early projective identification can be done in love or hate, and those early emotions affect the baby's approach to his exploring and perceiving reality – which is the beginning of learning.

In learning, or what Bion called 'K' activity, Bion brings together emotion and cognition, and he says this occurs always in a meaningful relationship between people, be it baby and parent in infancy, or patient and analyst in analysis. He differentiates 'K', or what he calls 'coming to know', from the acquisition of pieces of knowledge.

I will turn now to what Bion called 'minus K' – or reversal of learning'. Bion says, 'in minus K meaning is abstracted, leaving a denuded representation'. All the four examples I have given have a common striking characteristic, which is that by shifting the perspective, the interpretations have been denuded of meaning. Bion described the phenomenon of 'minus K' as not understanding or misunderstanding, and he linked it to primary envy. The infant because of his excessive envy of the breast does not experience mother's reverie as relief. On the contrary, by projecting this envy into the mother, what might have been relieving anxiety is experienced as mother taking his own value away.

The point I am making in this chapter is that the slicing-splitting is the basis of reversible perspective, which is the expression of as-if behaviour in analysis, and it is the result of the operation of minus K.

In the same chapters quoted earlier, Bion, when speaking about agreement and disagreement between patient and analyst, says, 'The principle should be that clinical observation must determine where the intersection of analyst's and patient's views is.' It is my point that the patient, by slicing the interpretation and thus changing the premisses, makes sure that such an intersection *does not take place*. Patient and analyst, though appearing to be together, do not make contact. It is precisely the contacting link which is cut, leaving the interpretation useless, repetitious, and empty.

The as-if patient cannot tolerate the analyst's interpretations, which he does not perceive as relieving or as conducive-to-growth. He resents them, feels them demeaning; he empties them of meaning, and uses them only to maintain a status quo. This envious reaction, I think, was clearly illustrated in patient C's dream about the sliced cake. Her mother was certainly a disturbed person (as were all the mothers of the four patients). But in the analysis, when the patient could feel the analyst as a better and more helpful object, and feel the possibility of liking and enjoying what she could get in the analysis, she was stopped by the hatred that originated in the fact that the analyst could get satisfaction from her (the patient's) relief and improvement. In the dream she did not want to get the bun (though she liked it) because 'the woman will enjoy the cream'.

The patients who predominantly use reversible perspective do not expect the analysis to be helpful for what it is. They do not learn from the analysis. They repeat with great frequency an attack on learning by denudation of meaning. They use projective identification with the analyst to mimic an analytic personality, misusing the interpretations. These feel useful for what they are not, or for whoever they are not meant to be for, but for themselves they are useless and despised.

The repetitive use of 'minus K' in analysis in my view not only repeats an early difficulty of the patient, but in the configuration of the 'as-if syndrome' is specifically designed to prevent the exploration of an internal situation. This situation is the consequence partially of an early operation of envy, partly of other developmental problems, and partly, too, connected with a specific maternal pathology, which in my experience has increased the child's early difficulties by stimulating a pseudo-adaptation.

In those patients there is a split between an ideal called 'The Analysis' and the actual analytic work. The ideal analysis is supposed to contain an unacknowledged disintegrated part, while the actual analytic work is felt to threaten this containment.

The slicing of the interpretations is, in my view, an attack on the dynamic link of the interpretation. It destroys the very meaning that the interpretation aims to convey. By severing this link, the analyst's interpretations become repetitions of empty statements, which, when not disposed of immediately, are heard by the patients as some kind of moral pronouncements.

It is difficult to grasp what is the subjective experience of the patient. Certainly, as I have said, he often seems to betray a sense of being morally judged. Patients seem often to convey an incessant sense of activity or busy-ness. There very rarely appears to be a spontaneous emotional response.

The phenomenon of 'slicing-splitting' is clinically observable, but it leaves me with many unresolved theoretical questions. One of them is: How does this type of splitting establish itself as a primary way of functioning?

In all the cases I have seen in which this phenomenon predominates I have found a puzzling balance between severe maternal (and often of both parents') pathology and a high endowment of envy. This balance seems to be more pronounced than in other kinds of patients with different types of defensive organizations.

Ross (1967) described a variety of as-if personalities. I prefer to call this an as-if analytical phenomenon, rather than an as-if personality. Certainly, the four patients I have described had very different personalities. For instance, patient A was the most ill of the four, and was closer to psychosis proper, while patient D would easily fall into the category of severe narcissistic personality.

The destruction of the internal coherence of the interpretation by breaking the meaningful links is triggered both by the hatred of the analyst, when the latter is able to provide understanding and to bring new meaning, and also by a dread of obtaining insight into a terrifying internal world. In this sense the 'slicing phenomenon' is at one and the same time a result of, and a defence against, envy. The type of denudation to which I am referring allows for some of the qualities (minimal as can be seen in the cake dream) of the experience to remain protected from further envious attacks, which would result in a more minute fragmentation. But the problems are never faced up to enough to be modified. To do this the patients would have to face what they did, and do, to their objects. They fear on the one hand that their external objects are beyond repair, and on the other they resent the help they need to get, to allow them to repair them.

In this sense the as-if syndrome, with its specific type of splittings, is a defensive organization formed to operate against awareness of and progress through the depressive position.

The as-if patients experience the awareness of their internal world as a menace to their sanity. They feel that they have (and had historically) only one of two ways of coping with this situation. Either they disintegrate completely, or they remain 'as-if'. The experience of not learning and being in analysis offers these patients a *modus vivendi*.

References

Abraham, K. (1924) 'A short study of the development of the libido, viewed in the light of mental disorders', in *Selected Papers on Psycho-Analysis*, London: Hogarth Press (1927), 418–501.

Anzieu, D. (1989) *The Skin Ego*, New Haven, CT: Yale University Press.

Arlow, J. and Brenner, C. (1969) 'The psychopathology of the psychoses: a proposed revision', *International Journal of Psycho-Analysis*, 50: 5–14.

Bick, E. (1968) 'The experience of the skin in early object relations', *International Journal of Psycho-Analysis*, 49: 484–6.

Bion, W.R. (1943) 'Intergroup tensions in therapy; their study as a task of the group', *Lancet*, 2, 27 Nov.

—— (1952) 'Group dynamics: a re-view', *International Journal of Psycho-Analysis*, 33: 235–47; also in M. Klein, P. Heimann, and R.E. Money-Kyrle (eds) *New Directions in Psycho-Analysis*, London: Tavistock Publications (1955), 440–77; paperback, Tavistock Publications (1971); also reprinted by Maresfield Reprints, London: H. Karnac Books (1985).

—— (1955) 'Language and the schizophrenic', in *New Directions in Psycho-analysis*, London: Tavistock Publications, 220–39.

—— (1957) 'The differentiation of the psychotic from the non-psychotic personalities', *International Journal of Psycho-Analysis*, 38: 266–75; also in *Second Thoughts*, London: Heinemann (1967), 43–64; reprinted in paperback, Maresfield Reprints, London: H. Karnac Books (1984); and in E. Bott Spillius (ed.) *Melanie Klein Today*, vol. 1, *Mainly Theory*, London: Routledge (1988), 61–78.

—— (1958) 'On arrogance', *International Journal of Psycho-Analysis*, 39: 144–6; and in *Second Thoughts*, London: Heinemann (1967), 86–92.

—— (1959) 'Attacks on linking', *International Journal of Psycho-Analysis*, 40: 308–15; also in *Second Thoughts*, London: Heinemann (1967), 93–100; and in E. Bott Spillius (ed.) *Melanie Klein Today*, vol. 1, *Mainly Theory*, London: Routledge (1988), 87–101.

—— (1961) *Experiences in Groups*, London: Tavistock Publications; and New York: Basic Books.

—— (1962a) 'A theory of thinking', *International Journal of Psycho-Analysis*, 43: 306–10; also in *Second Thoughts*, London: Heinemann (1967), 110–19; and in E. Bott Spillius (ed.) *Melanie Klein Today*, vol. 1, *Mainly Theory*, London: Routledge (1988), 178–86.

—— (1962b) *Learning from Experience*, London: Heinemann; reprinted in paperback, Maresfield Reprints, London: H. Karnac Books (1984).

—— (1963) *Elements of Psychoanalysis*, London: Heinemann; reprinted in paperback, Maresfield Reprints, London: H. Karnac Books (1984).

—— (1965) *Transformations*, London: Heinemann; reprinted in paperback, Maresfield Reprints, London: H. Karnac Books (1984).

—— (1967) 'Catastrophic change', unpublished paper.

—— (1970) *Attention and Interpretation*, London: Tavistock Publications; reprinted in paperback, Maresfield Reprints, London: H. Karnac Books (1984).

—— (1975) *A Memoir of the Future*, Book 1: *The Dream*, Rio de Janeiro: Imago.

—— (1977) *A Memoir of the Future*, Book 2: *The Past Presented*, Rio de Janeiro: Imago.

—— (1979) *A Memoir of the Future*, Book 3: *The Dawn of Oblivion*, Rio de Janeiro: Imago.

—— (1985) *The Long Week-End: 1897–1919*, edited by Francesca Bion, Oxford: Fleetwood Press.

Bollas, C. (1987) *The Shadow of the Object: Psychoanalysis of the Unthought Known*, London: Free Association Books.

Britton, R. (1986) 'The effects of serious parental psychological disturbances as seen in analysis'. Unpublished paper read to the British Psycho–Analytical Society, 4 June.

—— (1989) 'Projective identification: communication or evasion?' Unpublished paper given at the British Psycho-Analytical Society in Feb.

——, Feldman, M., and O'Shaughnessy, E. (1989) *The Oedipus Complex Today*, John Steiner (ed.), London: H. Karnac Books.

Deutsch, H. (1942) 'Some forms of emotional disturbance and their relationship to schizophrenia', *Psychoanalytic Quarterly*, 11: 301–21.

Freud, A. (1927) 'Introduction to technique of analysis of children', in *The Writings of Anna Freud*, London: Hogarth (1974), 3–72.

Freud, S. (1897a) Draft N, Letter 64, 31 May 1897. Extracts from the Fliess papers, *Standard Edition of the Complete Psychological Works of Sigmund Freud*, SE 1: 255.

—— (1897b) Letter 71, 15 Oct. 1897. Extracts from the Fliess papers, SE 1: 265.

—— (1909) *Analysis of a Phobia in a Five-Year-Old Boy*, SE 10: 3–149.

—— (1910) 'A special type of object-choice made by men', SE 11: 163–75.

—— (1916) 'The paths to symptom-formation', Lecture 23 of *Introductory Lectures on Psycho-Analysis*, SE 16: 358–77.

—— (1917) 'Mourning and melancholia', SE 14: 237–58.

—— (1918) *From the History of an Infantile Neurosis*, SE 17: 3–122.

—— (1920) *Beyond the Pleasure Principle*, SE 18: 3–61.

—— (1923a) *The Ego and the Id*, SE 19: 3–66.

—— (1923b) 'The infantile genital organization: an interpolation into the theory of sexuality', SE 19: 141–5.

—— (1924a) 'The dissolution of the Oedipus complex', SE 19: 173–9.

—— (1924b) 'The loss of reality in neurosis and psychosis', SE 19: 183–7.

—— (1925) 'Some psychical consequences of the anatomical distinction between the sexes', SE 19: 243–58.

—— (1933) 'Dreams and occultism', Lecture 30 of *New Introductory Lectures on Psycho-Analysis*, SE 22: 31–56.

—— (1939) *Moses and Monotheism*, SE 3: 3–137.

—— (1940) *An Outline of Psycho-Analysis*, SE 23: 141–207.

—— (1941) 'Findings, ideas, problems', SE 23: 299–300.

Frosch, J. (1983) *The Psychotic Process*, New York: International Universities Press.

Frosh, S. (1987) *The Politics of Psychoanalysis*, London: Macmillan.

Greenberg, J.R. and Mitchell, S. (1983) *Object Relations in Psychoanalytic Theory*, Cambridge, MA: Harvard University Press.

Greenson, R.R. (1974) 'Transference: Freud or Klein', *International Journal of Psycho-Analysis*, 55: 37–48.

Grinberg, L., Sor, D., and de Bianchedi, E.T. (1975) *Introduction to the Work of Bion*, trans. A. Hahn, Strathtay, Perthshire: Clunie Press.

Grosskurth, P. (1986) *Melanie Klein: her World and her Work*, New York: Alfred Knopf.

Grotstein, J.S. (1977) 'The psychoanalytic concept of schizophrenia: I. The dilemma; II. Reconciliation', *International Journal of Psycho-Analysis*, 58: 403–52.

—— (1981a) *Splitting and Projective Identification*, New York: Jason Aronson.

—— (1981b) 'Wilfrid R. Bion: the man, the psychoanalyst, the mystic', in J.S. Grotstein (ed.) *Do I Dare Disturb the Universe? a Memorial to Wilfrid R. Bion*, Beverly Hills: Caesura Press.

Heimann, P. (1950) 'On counter-transference', *International Journal of Psycho-Analysis*, 31: 81–4; also in P. Heimann, *About Children and Children-No-Longer: Collected Papers 1942–80*, Margret Tonnesmann (ed.), London: Routledge (1989).

Hinshelwood, R.D. (1989) *A Dictionary of Kleinian Thought*, London: Free Associations Press.

Hughes, J.M. (1989) *Reshaping the Psychoanalytic Domain*, Berkeley: University of California Press.

Isaacs, S. (1952) 'The nature and function of phantasy', in M. Klein, P.

Heimann, S. Isaacs, and J. Riviere, *Developments in Psycho-Analysis*, London: Hogarth Press, 67–121.

Jacobson, E. (1967) *Psychotic Conflict and Reality*, London: Hogarth Press.

Joseph, B. (1978) 'Different types of anxiety and their handling in the analytic situation', *International Journal of Psycho-Analysis*, 59: 223–8; and in Feldman, M. and Spillius, E. Bott (eds) *Psychic Equilibrium and Psychic Change: Selected Papers of Betty Joseph*, London: Routledge (1989), 106–15.

—— (1983) 'On understanding and not understanding: some technical issues', *International Journal of Psycho-Analysis*, 64: 291–8; also in *Psychic Equilibrium and Psychic Change: Selected Papers of Betty Joseph*, London: Routledge (1989), 139–50.

—— (1985) 'Transference: the total situation', *International Journal of Psycho-Analysis*, 66: 447–54; and in E. Bott Spillius (ed.) *Melanie Klein Today*, vol. 2, *Mainly Practice*, London: Routledge (1988), 61–72; and in *Psychic Equilibrium and Psychic Change: Selected Papers of Betty Joseph*, London: Routledge (1989), 156–67.

—— (1987) 'Projective identification: some clinical aspects', in J. Sandler (ed.) *Projection, Identification, Projective Identification*, Madison, CT: International Universities Press, 65–76; and in E. Bott Spillius (ed.) *Melanie Klein Today*, vol. 1, *Mainly Theory*, London: Routledge (1988), 138–50; also in *Psychic Equilibrium and Psychic Change: Selected Papers of Betty Joseph*, London: Routledge (1989), 168–80.

—— (1989) *Psychic Equilibrium and Psychic Change: Selected Papers of Betty Joseph*, M. Feldman and E. Bott Spillius (eds), London: Routledge.

Katan, M. (1979) 'Further exploration of the schizophrenic regression to the undifferentiated state', *International Journal of Psycho-Analysis*, 60: 145–74.

Kernberg, O. (1969) 'A contribution to the ego-psychological critique of the Kleinian school', *International Journal of Psycho-Analysis*, 50: 317–33.

—— (1975) *Borderline Conditions and Psychological Narcissism*, New York: Jason Aronson.

—— (1980) *Internal World and External Reality*, New York: Jason Aronson.

—— (1987) 'Projection and projective identification: developmental and clinical aspects', in J. Sandler (ed.) *Projection, Identification, Projective Identification*, Madison, CT: International Universities Press.

King, P. (1978) 'Affective response of the analyst to the patient's communication', *International Journal of Psycho-Analysis*, 59: 329–34.

King, P. and Steiner, R. (eds) (1990) *The Freud–Klein Controversies, 1941–45*, London: Routledge.

Klein, M. (1926) 'The psychological principles of early analysis', in *The Writings of Melanie Klein*, vol. 1, *Love, Guilt and Reparation*, London: Hogarth Press (1975), 128–38; also in paperback, New York: Dell Publishing Co. (1977).

—— (1927) 'Symposium on child analysis', in *The Writings of Melanie Klein*, vol. 1, *Love, Guilt and Reparation*, London: Hogarth Press (1975), 139–69.

—— (1928) 'Early stages of the Oedipus conflict', in *The Writings of Melanie Klein*, vol. 1, *Love, Guilt and Reparation*, London: Hogarth Press, 186–98.

—— (1930) 'The importance of symbol-formation in the development of the ego', *The Writings of Melanie Klein*, vol. 1, *Love, Guilt and Reparation*, London: Hogarth Press, 219–32.

—— (1932) 'The technique of early analysis', chap. 2 of *The Psycho-Analysis of Children*, vol. 2 of *The Writings of Melanie Klein*, London: Hogarth Press, 16–34.

—— (1935) 'A contribution to the psychogenesis of manic-depressive states', in *The Writings of Melanie Klein*, vol. 1, *Love, Guilt and Reparation*, London: Hogarth Press, 262–89.

—— (1940) 'Mourning and its relation to manic-depressive states', in *The Writings of Melanie Klein*, vol. 1, *Love, Guilt and Reparation*, London: Hogarth Press, 344–69.

—— (1945) 'The Oedipus complex in the light of early anxieties', in *The Writings of Melanie Klein*, vol. 1, *Love, Guilt and Reparation*, London: Hogarth Press, 370–419.

—— (1946) 'Notes on some schizoid mechanisms', in *The Writings of Melanie Klein*, vol. 3, *Envy and Gratitude and other Works*, London: Hogarth Press, 1–24.

—— (1952a) 'Some theoretical conclusions regarding the emotional life of the infant', in *The Writings of Melanie Klein*, vol. 3, *Envy and Gratitude and other Works*, London: Hogarth Press, 61–93.

—— (1952b) 'On observing the behaviour of young infants', in *The Writings of Melanie Klein*, vol. 3, *Envy and Gratitude and other Works*, London: Hogarth Press, 94–121.

—— (1955) 'The psycho-analytic play technique: its history and significance', in *The Writings of Melanie Klein*, vol. 3, *Envy and Gratitude and other Works*, London: Hogarth Press, 122–40.

—— (1957) *Envy and Gratitude*, in *The Writings of Melanie Klein*, vol. 3, *Envy and Gratitude and other Works*, London: Hogarth Press, 176–235.

—— (1959) 'Our adult world and its roots in infancy', in *The Writings of Melanie Klein*, vol. 3, *Envy and Gratitude and other Works*, London: Hogarth Press, 247–63.

—— (1960) *The Narrative of a Child Analysis*, Vol. 4 of in *The Writings of Melanie Klein*, London: Hogarth Press (1975).

London, N.J. (1973) 'An essay on psychoanalytic theory: two theories of schizophrenia. Part I: Review and critical assessment of the development of the two theories. Part II: Discussion and restatement of the specific theory of schizophrenia', *International Journal of Psycho-Analysis*, 54: 169–93.

Malin, A. and Grotstein, J.S. (1966) 'Projective identification in the therapeutic process', *International Journal of Psycho-Analysis*, 47: 43–67.

Marvell, A. (1681) 'A dialogue between the soul and body', in *Andrew*

Marvell: Selected Poetry and Prose, edited by Robert Wilcher, London: Methuen (1986).

Meisel, P. and Kendrick, W. (1986) *Bloomsbury/Freud: the Letters of James and Alix Strachey*, London: Chatto & Windus.

Meissner, W.W. (1980) 'A note on projective identification', *Journal of the American Psychoanalytic Association,* 28: 43–67.

—— (1987) 'Projection and projective identification', in J. Sandler (ed.) *Projection, Identification, Projective Identification*, Madison, CT: International Universities Press, 27–49.

Meltzer, D. (1978) 'The clinical significance of the work of Bion', Part III of *The Kleinian Development*, Strathtay, Perthshire: Clunie Press.

Mitchell, J. (1986) 'Introduction' to *The Selected Melanie Klein*, London: Penguin Books.

Money-Kyrle, R.E. (1956) 'Normal counter-transference and some of its deviations', *International Journal of Psycho-Analysis*, 37: 360–6; also reprinted in *The Collected Papers of Roger Money-Kyrle*, 1978, ed. D. Meltzer with the assistance of E. O'Shaughnessy, Strathtay, Perthshire: Clunie Press; reprinted also in E. Bott Spillius (ed.) *Melanie Klein Today*, vol. 2, *Mainly Practice*, London: Routledge (1988), 22–33.

Ogden, T. (1979) 'On projective identification', *International Journal of Psycho-Analysis*, 60: 357–73.

—— (1982) *Projective Identification and Psychotherapeutic Technique*, New York: Jason Aronson.

O'Shaughnessy, E. (1983) 'Words and working through', *International Journal of Psycho-Analysis*, 64: 281–9; also in E. Bott Spillius (ed.) *Melanie Klein Today*, vol. 2, *Mainly Practice*, London: Routledge (1988), 138–51.

—— (1989) 'Enclaves and excursions'. Unpublished paper given to the British Psycho-Analytical Society.

Pick, I. Brenman (1985) 'Working through in the counter-transference', *International Journal of Psycho-Analysis*, 66: 157–66; also in E. Bott Spillius (ed.) *Melanie Klein Today*, vol. 2, *Mainly Practice*, London: Routledge (1988), 34–47.

Rey, H. (1979) 'Schizoid phenomena in the borderline', in J. Le Boit and A. Capponi (eds), *Advances in the Psychotherapy of the Borderline Patient*, New York: Jason Aronson (1979), 449–84; also in E. Bott Spillius (ed.) *Melanie Klein Today*, vol. 1, *Mainly Theory*, London: Routledge (1988), 203–29.

Riesenberg Malcolm, R. (1970) 'The mirror: a perverse sexual phantasy in a woman seen as a defence against a psychotic breakdown', in E. Bott Spillius (ed.) *Melanie Klein Today*, vol. 2, *Mainly Practice*, London: Routledge (1988), 115–37.

Rosenfeld, H.A. (1950) 'Notes on the psychopathology of confusional states in chronic schizophrenia', in *Psychotic States*, London: Hogarth Press (1965), 52–62.

—— (1952) 'Notes on the psycho-analysis of the superego conflict of an acute schizophrenic patient', *International Journal of Psycho-Analysis*, 31: 111–31; also in *New Directions in Psycho-Analysis*, London: Tavistock (1955), 180–219; and in H. Rosenfeld, *Psychotic States*, London: Hogarth Press (1965), 63–103; also in E. Bott Spillius (ed.) *Melanie Klein Today*, vol. 1, *Mainly Theory*, London: Routledge (1988), 14–51.

—— (1954) 'Considerations regarding the psycho-analytic approach to acute and chronic schizophrenia', chap. 6 of *Psychotic States*, London: Hogarth Press, 117–27.

—— (1964) 'On the psychopathology of narcissism: a clinical approach', in *Psychotic States*, London: Hogarth Press, 169–79.

—— (1965) *Psychotic States*, London: Hogarth Press.

—— (1971) 'Contribution to the psychopathology of psychotic states: the importance of projective identification in the ego structure and object relations of the psychotic patient', in P. Doucet and C. Laurin (eds) *Problems of Psychosis*, vol. 1, The Hague: *Excerpta Medica*, 115–28; also in E. Bott Spillius (ed.) *Melanie Klein Today*, vol. 1, *Mainly Theory*, 117–37.

—— (1987) *Impasse and Interpretation*, London: Tavistock Publications.

Ross, N. (1967) 'The as-if concept', *Journal of the American Psychoanalytic Association*, 15: 59–81.

Sandler, J. (1976a) 'Dreams, unconscious fantasies and "identity of perception"', *International Review of Psycho-Analysis*, 3: 33–42.

—— (1976b) 'Countertransference and role responsiveness', *International Review of Psycho-Analysis*, 3: 43–7.

—— (1987a) (ed.) *Projection, Identification, Projective Identification*, Madison, CT: International Universities Press; first published in Great Britain by H. Karnac Books (1988).

—— (1987b) 'The concept of projective identification', in *Projection, Identification, Projective Identification*, Madison, CT: International Universities Press, 13–26.

—— and Sandler, A.M. (1978) 'On the development of object relationships and affects', *International Journal of Psycho-Analysis*, 59: 285–96.

Segal, H. (1950) 'Some aspects of the analysis of a schizophrenic', *International Journal of Psycho-Analysis*, 31: 268–78; also in *The Work of Hanna Segal*, New York: Jason Aronson (1981), 101–20; and in E. Bott Spillius (ed.) *Melanie Klein Today*, vol. 2, *Mainly Practice*, London: Routledge (1988), 96–114.

—— (1957) 'Notes on symbol formation', *International Journal of Psycho-Analysis*, 38: 391–7; and in *The Work of Hanna Segal*, New York: Jason Aronson (1981), 49–65; and in E. Bott Spillius (ed.) *Melanie Klein Today*, vol. 1, *Mainly Theory*, London: Routledge (1988), 160–77.

—— (1964) *An Introduction to the Work of Melanie Klein*, London: Heinemann; 2nd edn, London: Hogarth Press (1973).

—— (1973) *An Introduction to the Work of Melanie Klein*, 2nd edn, London: Hogarth Press.

—— (1979) *Klein*, London: Fontana/Collins.

Spillius, E. Bott (ed.) (1988) *Melanie Klein Today*, vol. 1, *Mainly Theory*, and vol. 2, *Mainly Practice*, London: Routledge.

Steiner, J. (1987) 'The interplay between pathological organizations and the paranoid-schizoid position', *International Journal of Psycho-Analysis*, 68: 69–80; also in E. Bott Spillius (ed.) *Melanie Klein Today*, vol. 1, *Mainly Theory*, London: Routledge (1988), 324–42.

—— (1990) 'Pathological organisations as obstacles to mourning: the role of unbearable guilt', *International Journal of Psycho-Analysis*, 71: 87–94.

Strachey, J. (1934) 'The nature of the therapeutic action of psycho-analysis', *International Journal of Psycho-Analysis*, 15: 275–93.

Wilcher, R. (ed.) (1986) *Andrew Marvell: Selected Poetry and Prose*, London: Methuen.

Williams, M.H. (1983) 'Underlying pattern in Bion's *A Memoir of the Future*', *International Review of Psycho-Analysis*, 10: 75–86.

Winnicott, D.W. (1960) 'Ego distortion in terms of true and false self', in *Maturational Processes and the Facilitating Environment*, London: Hogarth Press (1965), 140–52.

—— (1962) 'A personal view of the Kleinian contribution', in *The Maturational Processes and the Facilitating Environment*, London: Hogarth Press (1972).

Wordsworth, W. (1804) 'Ode' in *William Wordsworth*, Stephen Gill (ed.), Oxford University Press (1984).

Yorke, C. (1971) 'Some suggestions for a critique of Kleinian psychology', in *The Psychoanalytic Study of the Child*, 26: 129–55.

——, Wiseberg, S., and Freeman, T. (1989) *Development and Psychopathology: Studies in Psychoanalytic Psychiatry*, New Haven, CT: Yale University Press.

Name index

Abraham, K. 2, 3, 5
Anzieu, D. 103
Arlow, J. 9
Ascherson, Neal 27

Bick, Esther 103, 104
Bion, W.R. 6, 33, 36, 39, 48, 50, 51, 61, 76, 90, 92, 93, 96, 97, 104, 107, 110, 111, 115; career summary 8–10; container model 11–12, 102, 104–7, 109–12 *passim*; 'not learning' phenomenon 116–17, 118, 121–3 *passim*; on projective identification 61–3, 66–73 *passim*, 105, 122; on psychosis 9, 90–4, 96–8, 101; on sense of reality 40–1; on thinking/thought 9, 11, 39–40, 104–6; writing style of 12
Bollas, C. 62
Brenner, C. 9
Britton, R. 62, 110, 111

Deutsch, Helen 114

Ferenczi, S. 2
Freeman, T. 9
Freud, Anna 2, 15, 17
Freud, S. 2, 3, 15, 25, 52, 83; on instinct 20–1; on mourning 54; on Oedipus complex 34–6, 39; on psychosis 89–90
Frosch, J. 9

Frosh, S. 2

Greenberg, J.R. 2
Greenson, R.R. 2
Grinberg, L. 8
Grosskurth, P. 1, 2, 3
Grotstein, J.S. 8, 9, 63

Heimann, Paula 61
Hinshelwood, R.D. 1, 63
Hug-Hellmuth, Hildi 15
Hughes, J.M. 2

Isaacs, Susan 21, 25

Jacobson, E. 63
Jones, E. 2
Joseph, B. 8, 43, 47, 61, 76; on nudging 63; on projective identification 7, 63, 65–73 *passim*

Katan, M. 9
Kendrick, W. 3
Kernberg, O. 2, 63
King, P. 3, 78
Klein, M. 4, 9, 15, 28, 35, 36, 47, 51, 52, 53, 59–60, 75, 90, 120; career summary 1–4; child analysis and unconscious phantasy 14–23; early object relations 24–5, 28, 31, 33, 74–6; on mourning 55; Oedipus situation and depressive position 35–9, 45;

paranoid-schizoid vs. depressive position 5, 6, 46–56 *passim*; projective identification 59–61, 64–6, 75–6, 85–6; on psychosis 90; on relationship to analyst 4; on splitting 74–5

London, N.J. 9

Malin, A. 63
Marvell, Andrew 112–13
Meisel, P. 3
Meissner, W.W. 63
Meltzer, D. 8
Mitchell, J. 2, 21
Money-Kyrle, R.E. 61, 62, 69

Ogden, T. 63
O'Shaughnessey, E. 62, 63

Pick, I. Brenman 63

Rey, Henri 111
Rickman, John 8–9
Riesenberg Malcolm, R. 62

Rosenfeld, H.A. 8, 9, 31, 51, 61, 62, 76, 86, 97
Ross, N. 124

Sandler, A.M. 61
Sandler, J. 61, 63, 70, 83
Segal, H. 1, 8, 9, 14, 15–16, 21, 38, 40, 47, 50, 61, 76
Spillius, E. Bott 1, 61
Steiner, J. 55, 120
Steiner, R. 3
Strachey, Alix 2–3
Strachey, James 81

Trotter, Wilfred 8

Wilcher, R. 113
Williams, M.H. 8
Winnicott, Donald 35, 103, 115
Wiseberg, S. 9
'Wolf Man' 35–6
Wordsworth, W. 39

Yorke, C. 2, 9

Subject index

acting out, of analyst 63–4, 70–2
actualization (Sandler) 63, 83
Alpha elements (Bion) 105
ambivalence: and the depressive
    position 41, 48; normal splitting
    and 50
analyst: acting out by the 63–4, 70–2;
    experience of psychotic patients
    96–101 passim; as internal object
    33; and projective identification
    61, 87–8; see also analyst–patient
    relationship
analyst–patient relationship: and
    object relationships 4, 61; and
    patient psychosis 96–7; see also
    counter-transference, transference
annihilation, fear of 60
anxiety: depressive 5, 6; early
    Oedipal 28; and interpretation
    (children) 17–19 passim; normal
    splitting and 50; persecutory 6, 20,
    51; projection as defence against
    75; psychosis and (Klein) 90
'as-if' response to analysis 114–25;
    Bion on 116–17, 118, 121–3
    passim; as a defence 125; reversible
    perspective 116, 121–3; and slicing
    118–19, 123, 124; and splitting
    118, 124, 125

bereavement, see loss, mourning
Beta elements (Bion) 105

Bhagavadgita 8
bizarre objects (Bion) 51; psychosis
    and 93–4
breast: good and bad 24; introjection
    of 19

child drawings 32–3
child psychoanalysis: Anna Freud on
    17; clinical material 18–20 passim,
    25–7, 32–3, 43–5, 94–6; drawings
    in 32–3; early object relations
    25–7, 32–3; interpretation in
    17–18; Klein's play technique 3,
    14–19; toys in 15–16; transference
    in 15, 17; and unconscious
    phantasy 14–23 passim; see also
    depressive position, Oedipus
    situation
clinical material 21–2, 41, 42, 91;
    child analysis 18–20 passim, 25–7,
    32–3, 43–5, 94–6; container model
    (Bion) 102–12 passim; depressive
    position 41–5 passim; dreams 28,
    29–31, 49, 52, 55, 57, 65–6, 71,
    80–1, 118–21 passim; emergence
    of early object relations 25–33;
    mourning 56–8; 'Mrs A' (= Klein)
    55; 'not learning' phenomenon
    117–21; nudging 63;
    paranoid–schizoid position 49,
    51–2; 'Peter' (Klein) 16–17;
    projective identification 62–72,

76–88; psychosis 94–6, 98–101; 'Rita' (Klein) 15; splitting 76–88 *passim*

combined parental figure (Klein) 20, 28; defined 42

container model (Bion) 102, 104–7, 109–12 *passim*; clinical material 102–12 *passim*; father's role 110, 111; *see also* containment

containment 11–12, 109; parasitic/malignant 112; projective identification and 61–2; *see also* container model

counter-transference: Bion on 69; clinical material 100; Klein on 61; as projective identification 61–3; *see also* projective identification

defence: as-if phenomenon as 125; manic 58; paranoid-schizoid 6, 47; *see also* denial, depressive position, idealization, paranoid-schizoid position, projective identification, reaction formation, splitting

denial, of loss of object 52–3

depressive anxiety, *see* anxiety

depressive position 5, 6, 25, 48; clinical material 41–5 *passim*; differentiation within the 52–3, 60; Oedipus situation and the 34–45 *passim*

differentiation: in the depressive position 52–3, 60; in the paranoid-schizoid position 50; of self from object in mourning 54–5

drawings, child 32–3

dream material, *see* clinical material, dreams

ego: psychosis and 89–90; splitting of 6, 47, 75

empathy 76

envy: and as-if phenomenon 124; primary, and 'minus K' 122–3

excessive projective identification, *see* projective identification, excessive

father, and container model 110, 111

fragmentation, *see* pathological fragmentation

free association: play technique as 16, 17

frustration tolerance 11, 39–40; psychosis and 91, 93–4

guilt: in the depressive position 37, 39, 48; and interpretation 17

hallucinations: pathological fragmentation and 51

hallucinosis 99–100

hatred: child, re parental sexuality 36–7; of knowledge 42; –love balance 37, 45

idealization 31, 33, 115

instinct, Freud on 20–1

internal world 19–20, 61; as-if patient's 125; child's building up of 25

interpretation: in child analysis 17–19 *passim*; 'containing' 62; slicing of 124; of unconscious phantasy (Klein) 17

introjection: extractive (Bollas) 62; of mother's breast 19; phantasies of 6, 14; *see also* introjective identification

introjective identification 81–2

knowledge: and capacity to love 45; child's hatred of 42; infant development of (Bion) 106; *see also* learning

learning: Bion on 122; inhibition of desire for 36–7; lack of, in analysis 114–25 *passim*; *see also* knowledge

loss: and the depressive position 48; of loved object 53; reactivation of Oedipal 43; *see also* mourning

love, -and-hate balance 37, 45

minus K (Bion) 122–3
models: of projective identification
   63–4; *see also* container model
mourning 39; clinical material 56–8;
   in the depressive position 48, 52–8
   passim; and projective
   identification 54–5; *see also* loss

neurosis, vs. psychosis 89
nudging (Joseph) 7, 63, 64; clinical
   material 71

object: 'Alien' 111; analyst as internal
   33; bad, and psychosis 91;
   depressive position and 37, 39–40;
   idealized 31, 33; internal (child's)
   17; Klein on 5, 74–6; loss of loved
   53; persecutory, and psychosis 10;
   splitting of 6, 47, 50, 52; *see also*
   primary objects, bizarre objects
object relations(hips) 24–33; and
   analyst–patient relationship 4;
   clinical material on early 25–33; in
   paranoid-schizoid position 47; and
   perception 24; splitting and (Klein)
   74–6
obsessional/compulsive behaviour:
   depressive position and 36–8
   passim; *see also* repetition
   compulsion
Oedipus situation 34–45 *passim*;
   Freud on 34–6, 39; Klein's
   re-dating of 22, 28, 36

paranoid-schizoid position 6, 25, 47,
   59; clinical material 49, 51–2;
   defences in the 6, 60;
   differentiation in the 50;
   pathological fragmentation 50–1;
   perception of parental sexuality in
   41–3; transition to depressive
   position 120
parental sexuality; child's hatred of
   36–7; perception of, in
   paranoid-schizoid position 41–2;
   phantasies of 37–8, 41–3; *see also*

combined parental figure, Oedipus
   situation
pathological fragmentation 50–1
patient–analyst relationship, *see*
   analyst–patient relationship
persecutor, internal 60
phantasies: Klein's concept of 21;
   about mother's body 20; Oedipal
   23, 40, 45; omnipotent 85–6; of
   parental intercourse 37–8, 41–3; of
   projection into the object 6;
   projective identification as 61; in
   young children 3; *see also*
   unconscious phantasy
play technique 3, 14–19; as free
   association 16, 17
preconception (Bion) 36, 39
primary objects 3, 4; ambivalence
   towards 48; infant's 25; projective
   identification and 61; splitting of 31
projection: of bad experiences 10,
   74, 75; phantasies of 6; vs.
   projective identification 63, 73; *see*
   also projective identification
projective identification 6, 7, 32;
   acquisitive (Britton) 62; analyst's
   experience of 61–4, 70–2, 87–8;
   Bion's 'model' 61–3, 65–73 *passim*,
   105, 122; clinical experience of
   63–73, 76–88; clinical models of
   63–4; in depressive position 53;
   evacuation vs. communication in
   86–7; 'excessive' (Klein) 60–1, 92;
   Joseph's 'model' 63, 65–6, 70–3;
   Klein's 'model' 59–61, 64–6,
   75–6, 85–6; normal vs.
   pathological 61–2; in
   paranoid-schizoid position 47; as
   phantasy 61; vs. projection 63, 73;
   reversal of in mourning 54–5; and
   technique 62–3
psychoanalytic technique, *see*
   technique
psychosis 89–101; analyst's
   experience of patient 96–7; Bion
   on 9, 90–4, 96–8, 101; clinical

material 94–6, 98–101; Freud on
89–90; Klein on 90; vs. neurosis
89; persecutory objects and 10;
and projective identification 96,
97; and therapeutic change 97–8;
transference psychosis 97

reaction formation 82
reality principle 89; psychosis and
90–1
reparative wishes 36, 37, 48
repetition compulsion 83
reversible perspective (Bion) 116,
121–3

splitting: breakdown of 51; clinical
material 76–88 *passim*; of ego 6,
47, 75; Klein on 74–5; normal 50,
60; in 'not learning' 118, 124, 125;
of object 6, 47; off of Oedipal
romance 40; of primary object 31
superego: early (Klein) 3, 17, 20, 23;
ego-destructive (Bion) 107
symbol formation 21, 48; failure of

37, 38, 40, 47
symbolic equations (Segal) 40, 47

technique: play technique (Klein) 3,
14–19; projective identification
and 62–3
therapeutic change: lack of in analysis
114–25 *passim*; psychosis and 97–8
thinking: Bion's model of 9, 11, 39,
104–6; confusion with
symbolization 40, 47; psychosis
and 92, 97–8
toys, in child analysis 15–16
transference: in child analysis 15, 17,
25; *see also* transference psychosis
transference psychosis (Rosenfeld) 97

unconscious (the): Klein's view of
25; *see also* unconscious phantasy
unconscious phantasy 14–23 *passim*;
interpretation of 17; Klein's
concept of 20–1; play as 17;
projective identification as 85–6